A
Military Leadership
Notebook

A
Military Leadership
Notebook
Principles into Practice

Walter F. Ulmer Jr.
Lieutenant General, US Army (Retired)
Former President and CEO, Center for Creative Leadership
With Foreword by General Barry R. McCaffrey

⊙ iUniverse®

A MILITARY LEADERSHIP NOTEBOOK
PRINCIPLES INTO PRACTICE

iUniverse books may be ordered through booksellers or by contacting:

iUniverse
1663 Liberty Drive
Bloomington, IN 47403
www.iuniverse.com
1-800-Authors (1-800-288-4677)

Because of the dynamic nature of the Internet, any web addresses or links contained in this book may have changed since publication and may no longer be valid. The views expressed in this work are solely those of the author and do not necessarily reflect the views of the publisher, and the publisher hereby disclaims any responsibility for them.

Any people depicted in stock imagery provided by Thinkstock are models, and such images are being used for illustrative purposes only.
Certain stock imagery © Thinkstock.

ISBN: 978-1-5320-2675-1 (sc)
ISBN: 978-1-5320-2674-4 (e)

Library of Congress Control Number: 2017912431

Print information available on the last page.

iUniverse rev. date: 11/08/2017

Comments on the book

"General Walt Ulmer shares a lifetime of living, learning and observing leadership on the battlefield, at the highest levels of the United States Army, and across large organizations and corporations. Through observations, stories, useful checklists, and practical suggestions, Walt Ulmer has provided a leadership notebook to be devoured with a highlighter and handwritten notes in the margin — these are lessons one can return to often."

Frank C. Sullivan, Chairman and CEO, RPM International, Inc.

··········

"We need to make sure the next generations of military leaders are exposed to this *Notebook*. It is an invaluable contribution to understanding the practical application of leadership principles. General Ulmer takes us through his journey by weaving together the best leadership practices he lived, both as senior military officer and CEO. His innovative tools, checklists, and concepts provide a clear, compelling, and remarkable resource invaluable to both military leaders and the ranks of the corporate world."

John F. Campbell, General, U.S. Army (Retired). Former Vice Chief of Staff and former Commander, U.S. Forces, Afghanistan.

··········

"General Ulmer's wisdom and tested experience form the essence of this exceptional work. He reveals managerial best practice and adds authenticity from proven leadership in both military and academic settings. His perspective, advice, and recommendations are valuable in all sectors of our society. Leaders who choose to be relevant in the 21st Century need to put this book high on their reading list."

David M. Noer, DBA, Professor Emeritus of Business Leadership, Elon University. His books include *Healing the Wounds: Overcoming the Trauma of Business* Layoffs (1998 and 2016) and *Revitalizing Downsized Organizations* (2015.)

Comments on the book

"This book is nothing less than a gift from General Walt Ulmer, a guru on leadership in organizations. It is that rarest of rarities—a marvelous blend of a lifetime of real-world experience and decades of tutoring, all presented in clear prose. It is unique, so distinct as to all but defy definition among the daunting list of other volumes on the topic. Ulmer labels it merely a "cook book" on organizational leadership. If so, he is the quintessential master chef. This book, a lasting legacy, should be in the knapsack of each new lieutenant, on the desks of all generals, and in the hands of everyone in between."

Dave R. Palmer, Lieutenant General, U.S. Army (Retired), former Superintendent, West Point. His books include *George Washington and Benedict Arnold* (2006), and *1794: America, Its Army, and the Birth of the Nation (1994).*

··········

"Every day at every location around the world where Army units serve, their leaders almost singularly will determine if our Soldiers and civilians serve proudly in an esteemed military profession, or whether they are just cogs in another big government bureaucracy. Leaders who follow the proven insights that Walt Ulmer has gathered for this book have a far better chance of maintaining the standards and traditions of Army professionalism, and the resulting effectiveness on which our republic depends."

Don M. Snider, PhD, retired Army officer, is Project Director of "The Future of the Army Profession" and a recognized leader on Army professionalism

Comments on the book

"A Leadership Notebook: Putting Principles into Practice, is the most useful and comprehensive book on the theory, art, and practice of leadership that I have read in my thirty years of active Army service and my twenty years as a military historian. No one is as well suited for writing a military leadership manual. This book captures the fertile intersection of sound leadership theory and the demands of day to day operations. It is not a stretch to consider it in its field a work of practical genius."

James Scott Wheeler, PhD, Colonel U.S. Army (Retired) is a former professor of history at the U.S. Military Academy. His books include *Jacob L. Devers: A General's Life,* and *The Big Red One: America's Legendary 1ˢᵗ Infantry Division from World War I to Desert Storm.*

· · · · · · · · · ·

"Service has been at the heart of Walt Ulmer's remarkable career, and this book is his newest contribution to making the world a better place. The thought-provoking, practical wisdom that Walt draws from his military experiences will be of great benefit to business, education, and nonprofit leaders as well. His advice can accelerate our personal effectiveness and elevate performance in every sector."

John Ryan, Vice Admiral, USN, (Retired) is President and CEO of the Center for Creative Leadership and former Superintendent of the U.S. Naval Academy.

· · · · · · · · · ·

"All good leaders will embrace lessons found in this superb compilation of thoughts written by a true master of the art. Anybody reading what he writes will be the better for it. I remain in awe of his leadership techniques. The best year of my thirty-year Army career was spent beside Walt Ulmer."

John C. Bahnsen, Brigadier General, U. S. Army (Retired), is the highly-decorated Author of *American Warrior: A Combat Memoir of Vietnam.*

Comments on the book

"This document contains a lifetime of wisdom, with an unusual way of thinking about the executive's world. While generally well-schooled on governance and business models, senior leaders are often lacking in deep understanding of organizational systems. Consequently, most large-scale organizations are unaware of the waste of precious energy arising from systemic disconnects.

In this book, Walt Ulmer shows how executives should think about these systems, and describes tools leaders can use to look for the "energy leaks" that sap organizational vigor and discourage subordinate engagement. While this book should be required reading for leaders at all levels, mastering its concepts is critical at the top. While many can "*see*" dysfunction, only senior executives can both "*see*" and "*fix*.""

T. O. Jacobs, PhD, is a former executive at the Army Research Institute for the Behavioral and Social Sciences, and for years a consultant to the Army on assessment and training. A former Distinguished Visiting Professor of Behavioral Science at the Industrial College of the Armed Forces, he is Senior Fellow, Executive Leadership Assessment and Development, the RBL Group.

Contents

Part 3
Critical Leader Behaviors

Part 4
Reinforcing and Respecting the Chain of Command

Part 5
Organizational Climates and Trust

Part 6
Managing Organizations and Leading Staffs

Part 7
Following, Learning, Teaching, and Serving

Charts

Appendices

Foreword

A Military Leadership Notebook: Principles into Practice by Lieutenant General Walter Ulmer is the most useful single work on getting organizations to function effectively that I have read in many years. In running both military and civilian enterprises, I have been exposed to extensive formal leadership training and individual coaching. The huge value of this work by General Ulmer is not theory of leadership—it is practice. This *Notebook* has tools a leader can pick up and use. They are time-tested.

With clarity of expression and logic, it is devoid of jargon. It is a "cookbook" of lessons from the author's thirty-three years in uniform as a leader at every level of the U.S. Army, followed by ten years as CEO of the world-renowned Center for Creative Leadership.

Walt Ulmer was an icon of positive leadership and fundamental integrity during his years as a military leader. I first encountered him during the mid-1970s when he served as commandant of cadets at West Point. I was a young officer teaching comparative politics and U.S. government in the Department of Social Sciences.

General Ulmer was widely respected as a rock of common sense and personal moral courage during one of the worst periods in the history of our Army. The disastrous Vietnam War, with 350,000 killed and wounded, was drawing to a sad end. The country was divided and angry. Young officers on the West Point faculty were embittered with our failed military and political leadership. The Army had lost its way.

A handful of young generals—of whom Walt Ulmer was one of the most respected—helped us find our direction and capture again the values that made the armed forces the most respected institution in America. I was unsurprised to see him go on to very senior military rank and become the most respected voice in a beleaguered military institution trying to rediscover its moral footing.

There is an inspirational historical story to be told of how our armed forces regained control of their destiny and purpose. This successful transformation started with a great deal of introspection and analysis by senior military leaders. We had to discover our historical values and regain our confidence.

General Ulmer became a steady voice and guide in that process. More importantly, he didn't just think and write about leadership—he was personally on the line as an operational unit commander at almost every level in peace and war. His personal courage (twice awarded the Silver Star for valor) and effectiveness on combat tours lent huge credibility to his writing and teaching efforts about leadership.

As you read this compelling book, you will be struck by its common sense and utility. Although General Ulmer presents this book as a teaching tool for military leaders, I would argue that it has equal relevance and value to civilian business executives. I now have fifteen years' experience in helping manage and govern large civilian organizations, both commercial and nonprofit. At the end of the day, leadership is everything.

The only reality in business organizations is the work and creativity of the dozens or thousands of employees. There will be no successful outcomes unless executives motivate and lead the business teams to produce value for clients. Nothing happens by accident in real life. Success requires dedicated leaders operating on principles outlined in this superb piece. The stakes for business may not be life or death, as they are in military units in combat, but the outcomes will be unmistakably rewarding or painfully remembered.

Part of the fascination of this *Leadership Notebook* is how it weaves together real-world experience with sophisticated studies and findings forged from Walt Ulmer's years of experience as the CEO of the prestigious Center for Creative Leadership. There is no question that scientific measurement and analysis can tease the truth from observation and data. I have been fortunate to twice attend leadership development sessions at the Center—once as a young captain and again as a new brigadier general. I can honestly say they were both life-changing experiences. The wealth of knowledge Walt Ulmer acquired at CCL is woven into this leadership tutorial.

There is a lot to be learned here. Whether you are a Ranger battalion commander, the executive chairman of a giant corporation, or the CEO of a not-for-profit, you will be intrigued by lessons on creating trust; measuring leadership climate and culture; toxic leadership; keeping senior leaders immersed in reality; eliminating "dumb stuff"; empowerment and decentralization; inspecting the inspectors; and using survey and performance data wisely.

You the reader will encounter here innovative tools, checklists, and concepts that any executive team will value. This superb book outlines how to lead a collection of people to creatively, proudly, and cooperatively focus on the assigned objectives. We should be grateful that Walt Ulmer has pulled all this together.

Barry R. McCaffrey
General, U.S. Army (Retired)

Acknowledgments

There are hundreds of people over the eight-plus decades of my life who have contributed generously to the experiences that led me to put these notes together. To all of them, I owe a debt. Some were family members. Some were formal teachers. Some were bosses in military or civilian organizations, and some were peers and colleagues. Many were subordinate to me in the organization but instructors in fact. I wish I had taken the time to be sure all of them knew of my appreciation for their friendship and coaching.

Having been a teacher myself at times, I know teachers learn at least as much as students. Now, after composing this book, I recognize that authors may gain more than readers.

I thank in particular these individuals who took the special effort to review and comment on various drafts or portions thereof: Mike Adler, Doc Bahnsen, Barry Berglund, Craig Bullis, Tom Cole, *Bob Cone*, Mal Craig, Lauren Dobel, Marlene Douglas, Jim Dozier, Owen Jacobs, *Fred Long*, Rick Lynch, David Noer, Dave Palmer, Marvin Pinson, Roy Ray, George Reed, Mike Shaler, Mike Sirkis, Perry Smith, Mac Snodgrass, Bob Sorley, Bill Sternbergh, Frank Sullivan, *Heath Twichell*, Rebekah Ulmer, Danielle Villlanueva, Scott Wheeler, Greg Wilcox, Paul Wilcox and Jack Woodmansee. Special thanks to my personal editor and principal assistant for this and six decades of other projects, Marty UImer, whose support along with that of Buck, Jeff, and Tom has been unfailing.

I appreciate also the special contributions of these diligent, perceptive proofreaders: Alex, Bennett, Catherine, Maria, Lexi, and Jeff.

Introduction

The prevailing global scenario spells danger for all but well-led institutions. Only organizations with competent, visionary, and thoughtful leaders can survive the challenges from every direction: political, economic, and ideological. With that in mind, this notebook offers observations, techniques, suggestions, and conclusions gathered from six decades of practice and study. It is filled with preferences, biases, and lessons learned. All are related to creating climates in which leaders at all levels can lead, organizations can succeed, and talented people are encouraged to serve in institutions that shape our world.

This notebook is more cookbook than novel. Like a cookbook, it aims to produce a useful product. Also like a cookbook, it is not rigidly organized. It swings back and forth from simple ingredients to complex sauces; from frying eggs to creating Thanksgiving dinner. It has lists and tables—not glamorous, but useful. All recipes have been tested. It repeats ingredients and may be a monument to redundancy. The chef picks the recipes that will best serve the occasion.

Unlike typical cookbooks, however, these notes offer suggestions on what chefs might do to improve their performance; thoughts on why some meals didn't turn out well; and options for redesign of the whole kitchen. In some parts critical of current institutional practice, it seeks to be useful in a wide range of settings. It should be helpful to the aspiring cook and to the four-star chef.

Thousands of books have explored military leadership: how it's defined; how or if combat and garrison leadership differ; how it changes from tactical to strategic; how or if it can be taught; how it can be evaluated; how technology might influence its application; how different subordinates may require different approaches; how leaders without positional authority rely on motivational skills; why "great captains" have succeeded or failed; and even, in some academic circles, whether or not leaders make a difference. Leaders in fact remain a major element of sustained combat power—or any other kind of organizational power.

Becoming an effective leader depends significantly more on how to apply principles than on knowing them. Moving from informed good intentions to constructive behavior is the solution. Both how to get the job done and getting it done are important. Defining the job is crucial. That "job" rightly includes responsibility for tomorrow as well as today. A sense of ownership for outcomes, intentional and otherwise, should be lurking behind every leader's decisions and personal example.

Many of the concepts presented in this book are relevant to platoon exercises at the national training centers, leading a battalion against an enemy-held village in a distant desert or jungle, creating a supportive climate at Camp Swampy, or starting a business in Wichita. Some specifics in these notes are more relevant to the world of the lieutenant than to that of the general, and vice versa. But since all generals were once lieutenants and all lieutenants have some chance at becoming generals, there should be utility for each in visiting both worlds.

This discussion emphasizes practical steps to build high-performing organizations. Leaders may deal with different realms of complexity, but every leader articulates goals; clarifies directives; focuses effort; earns trust; builds and motivates teams; sets the example for professional behavior; sustains a supportive working environment; and, if necessary, rationalizes sacrifice and keeps hope alive. While context does matter, principles have universal application as long as humans are collectively involved in pursuing a goal.

This notebook includes criticism of selected processes and policies, and suggests changes. Institutional response to the need for change involving organizational climates and personnel policies is notably slow. This is in part due to the comparative reality that budget deficiencies, accident rates, and even ground tactics are observable, usually measurable, and only moderately emotional. The health of command climates, a more complex and ambiguous target, involves tradition, culture, and human aspirations.

The extent to which leaders are made versus born has been a longstanding debate. It is obviously some of both. However, the opportunities and limitations in modifying outlook, attitude, and behavior through indoctrination and education deserve realistic appraisal. There are limits to what can be done to alter the hard-wiring of genetics and the branding of early childhood experience. We often expect more from developmental interventions than organizations can deliver. However, working from a baseline of reasonable intellect and healthy ego, much can be done to enhance leadership skills. We do have in our society abundant natural talent for handling all sorts of contingencies. The challenge is to identify, attract, appreciate, and nurture that talent for the benefit of the institution and the nation it proudly supports.

The American military has been a producer of versatile leaders for all of it existence. The magnitude of its WWII performance was stunning. Growing an army from 188,000 in 1939 (19th in the world in size) to 8.3 million in 1945 was in itself a near miracle. It was accomplished in great part by the leadership of thousands of young graduates from training centers such as the Officer Candidate School (OCS) at Fort Benning, Georgia. Management guru Dr. Warren Bennis, a 1942 OCS graduate, remarked that in all his formal education nothing equaled what he learned at Fort Benning and later applied as a company commander in combat in Europe.

Proper leadership—at the top or throughout the organization—is of course not the only contributor to productivity. At its best, leadership by itself cannot guarantee results. Vision, motivation, timely decisions, and mutual trust--powerful as they are-- have their limits. Organizational efficiency and effectiveness require both human talent and material resources. A supportive macro-environment also helps.

The ideas supporting this book began in 1952, when I first put together notes preparing for a tour as a platoon leader in Korea (I arrived about the time the truce was signed). I was still making notes for Pentagon and Army War College discussions in 2016.

While weaponry and materiel have changed dramatically in those sixty years, human aspiration and interaction not so much. We still learn from Trafalgar, Valley Forge, Little Round Top, Bastogne, and Heartbreak Ridge. While the future may see national military power relying increasingly on virtual-reality, cyber-driven, robotic-encounters, leadership will never go out of style. Whether engaged in hand-to-hand combat or remote targeting, the practitioners will be members of organizations dependent on leaders to educate, train, protect, nurture, and inspire. The dynamics of command climates will be relevant as long as humans form groups dedicated to accomplishing missions, and crucial beyond relevant if those missions have noble purpose.

Among my many good fortunes was joining the Center for Creative Leadership as its president and CEO after military retirement. CCL is an international nonprofit organization devoted to leadership education, behavioral science research, and executive development. It was an enjoyable, challenging, and productive nine-plus years working with some of the world's foremost practitioners in those disciplines.

My experience at CCL, followed by a few years as an independent consultant, produced one mild surprise and confirmed one assumption. The surprise was that while we in the military have a less-than-perfect institution, our concepts, values, and practices look as good as anything around. The confirmed assumption was that all individuals who are steeped in the culture of western civilization need and increasingly expect thoughtful leadership.

This notebook is centered on the world of commissioned officers in military organizations. While there are thought leaders, scientific leaders, art world leaders, and PTA leaders whose contributions to society are enormous, the focus here is on leaders who have formal authority in traditional organizations. In the military, as elsewhere, much of the leading is done by those lower in the chain of command. The noncommissioned officer corps of American military organizations represents the core of direct leadership. Their values, ideals, and principles are at the heart of the institution. The context of their leadership is somewhat different from that of the officer leader and as such not directly discussed in this book. But no commissioned officer in the American military has ever succeeded, in war or peace, without the support and leadership of professional noncommissioned officers.

While the essentials of leadership pertain in all hierarchical organizations, we in the military are in some respects different. Military members are on call 24-7, available for urgent global missions without consultation, and can't walk off the job. Military leaders have been granted authority by their government to command, reward, and punish. And the military culture recognizes that in some situations life must be sacrificed to accomplish the mission. My biased conclusion remains that America's military presents a combination of integrity and commitment rarely found in our world.

Walt Ulmer

Greensboro, North Carolina, and New Harbor, Maine

3 June, 2017

PART 1

Definitions, Principles, and Other Generalities

The principles of leadership do not change ... they were in effect when Caesar exhorted his troops ... although it took 1,900 years to refine and measure the concepts.

Bernard M. Bass, PhD

What Do We Mean by Leadership?

The words *leader* and *commander* are powerful. This seems true across cultures and ages. Within formal organizations like the military, individuals in charge rely on two sources of authority to get the job done: granted statutory power and personal power which is gained by earning trust. Good leaders use both.

Leadership and management are different but so imprecisely defined and so entwined in practice that spending time on any leader-versus-manager argument may not be productive. The essence of leadership is vision, motivation, and trust; the heart of management is goal-setting, resource allocation, and work prioritization. Organizational leaders must allocate as well as motivate, defining the task while articulating the vision. Perhaps *responsibleship* might better describe the task of accomplishing organizational goals. General Bruce Clarke, a major contributor to discussions of organizational leadership, promoted the terms *generalship* and *commandership* in his writings. However, *leadership* seems good enough for our purposes.

A 2015 Army textbook and excellent basic reference, *ADMP (or FM) 6-22, Leader Development,*[1] defines leadership as "the process of influencing people by providing purpose, direction, and motivation to accomplish the mission and improve the organization." That last phrase, "improve the organization," was added about ten years

---

[1] This basic U.S. Army reference provides remarkably comprehensive coverage of leadership theory and practice.

ago. It reminds us that an organizational leader's responsibilities extend beyond the current mission and horizon.

Just for the record, here are a few other definitions of leadership, with my comments:

- "A leader is a dealer in hope" (Napoleon). While true, this definition focuses only on a leader's need to engage the emotional or affective component.

- "If your actions inspire others to dream more, to learn more, do more, and become more, you are a leader" (John Quincy Adams). Adams is describing a leader and not the process of leadership. He covers all the bases except the critical need to describe the goal.

- "A leader is best when people barely know he exists, not so good when people obey and acclaim him, worst when they despise him … But of a good leader, who talks little, when his work is done, his aim fulfilled, they will say, 'We did it ourselves'" (Lao Tzu, sixth-century BC). This may describe the perfect leader. Considering human ambition and the lure of visible accomplishment, however, it is a bit idealistic.

- "Leadership is the incremental influence that a person has beyond his or her formal authority" (Vecchio). This definition represents what might be described as pure leadership. Its execution relies on respect and trust without recourse to formal authority. It is the leader mode in the PTA and other volunteer groups. It inadequately defines organizational leadership.

- "My definition of a leader … is a man who can persuade people to do what they don't want to do or to do what they're too lazy to do, and like it" (Harry Truman). I admired Truman's decision-making and acceptance of responsibility along with his strategic vision that uplifted the cultures of Germany and Japan. But any assumption of soldier reluctance or laziness does not suit a volunteer organization. My experience with draftees was that most of them wanted to do good work and responded well to competent leaders. How to integrate formal authority with the earned power of mutual trust remains an issue.

- "Actions that focus resources to create desirable opportunities" (David P. Campbell). My friend Dr. Campbell captures the essence of leadership in a few words. The "focusing resources" part highlights the reality that leading requires more than motivating. But as Dr. Campbell appreciates, our mission is often more complex than a "desirable opportunity."
- "Leadership is a process of giving purpose (meaningful direction) to collective effort, and causing willing effort to be expended to achieve purpose" (T. O. Jacobs). Dr. Jacobs has been contributing to Army leadership studies and doctrine for many years; his writings are definitive and compelling. His "willing effort" is fundamental. "Unwilling" does not last very long.
- As some old sergeant said, "A good leader can step on your boots without spoiling the shine!"

Tweaking definitions has limited practicality. It is worth some effort, because it provokes thought on the essence of the topic. My own definition of organizational leadership is "a process in which an individual provides direction, motivation, and resources to accomplish a mission."

I don't like to use *the leadership* as a noun meaning the few people at the top of an organization, as though that cluster of individuals were a leader. Nor do I think that *the leadership team* as a title makes much sense. Leadership is the activity of one person who has responsibility for decision-making at a particular organizational level. Effective leaders build teams, engage others, use available experience, and share authority. But they cannot share ultimate responsibility. People need to know who they work for. The public needs to know who is responsible. Troikas rarely succeed.

Anyone who causes others to do the right thing is a leader. Anonymous

Note
2

Thoughts, Assumptions, and Biases

- Our institutional memory is short. We keep reinventing parts of the leadership wheel. Although this gives each generation a chance to discover, react, and create, relearning consumes enormous organizational energy. Preserving lessons from experience and embedding them in the culture remains a challenge.

- Good people need guidance on what to do, but considerable leeway in how to do it. Attending simultaneously to these different needs is a primary leadership challenge.

- Organizational leaders at every level are confronted with competition between the needs of today and those of tomorrow. Today's needs can overwhelm regard for tomorrow.

- Left unchallenged, centralization always wins over empowerment, with the resulting compromise of optimum organizational performance.

- We typically underestimate the competence, commitment, and wisdom of young people and rarely make optimal use of their potential.

- As we move to the higher ranks, we should spend more time praising good work than worrying about details others can attend to. There is something good in every organization. Authentic praise and cheerleading lifts all boats.

- The default setting for all organizations is "stupid." Leaders must continuously inject coherence, rationality, common sense, and hope. Humor also helps.

- Measuring and reporting individual and organizational effectiveness is the most neglected and underappreciated aspect of organizational leadership.

- Taking appropriate action against a friend or colleague who has demonstrated unprofessional behavior is a difficult task. For an organizational leader, it is also an essential one. Perhaps even more difficult is informing a loyal, hard-working subordinate that he is not being recommended for further promotion.

- If a picture is worth a thousand words, a living example is worth ten-thousand.

- Every decision involves a degree of risk. We need to explore the genesis of leader risk-aversion, a pernicious condition not uncommon in hierarchical organizations.

- Both development and selection deserve attention, but we expect too much from leader development and undervalue the criticality of leader selection.

- It is much easier for a leader to fix a broken system than to sustain excellence in a good one. Fixing is more easily noticed and rewarded.

- People are basically good and, absent contrary evidence, should be trusted. But at every age we remain susceptible to temptations that can divert us from professional behavior.

- When a respected boss-or coach or teacher-shows confidence in our future success it is a powerful, memorable moment.

- Poor leaders always seem to have too much authority; good leaders never seem to have enough. The solution lies more in leader selection than in authority redistribution.

- The line between productive self-confidence and dysfunctional arrogance is mighty slim, as it is between healthy ambition and unseemly self-promotion.

- Unethical behavior in organizations arises more often from dumb policies than from individual character defects. It cannot be forgiven, but it can many times be prevented.

- High-tech communication and data manipulation represent both a boon and a threat to leader effectiveness. Leaders have to be alert to depersonalization.

- I have never known personally a really good leader without a sense of humor.

- Personality—an individual's style and likeability—plays a powerful role. Major commanders in strategic campaigns are too often chosen on friendship rather than past performance.
- If we want a reliable assessment of leader competence and character, we must consider the views of subordinates.
- The contemporary American military, with all its imperfections, is among the most integrity-driven institutions on earth. It strives to be a true meritocracy in an era where well-meaning societal transformation sometimes complicates that process.
- Leaders are not miracle-workers. Extraordinary vision, gifted intellect, emotional resilience, boundless energy, relevant experience, and good intentions can't get the job done without adequate resources, and often without public support.

From its infancy, the study of history has been the study of leaders— what they did and why they did it. Bernard M. Bass, PhD[2]

---

[2] Bernard Bass produced seminal works on transformational leadership. He led several studies of Army leadership, one of which is noted in the reference list.

What Do Leaders Do?

The short answer is: get the job done. Then, however, we need to define the job. All leaders have two distinct, overlapping, competing jobs. The first is to accomplish the assigned mission ("Enter the continent of Europe and defeat the Axis armies" or "Take Hill 671" or "Keep the helicopter fleet at 80 percent readiness" or "Support the blood drive"). The second is to keep a reserve for the next battle and ensure the future health of the institution. "Future health of the institution" includes enforcing professional standards and developing leaders.

The dilemma of accomplishing today's mission versus attending to future needs of the institution plays out at all organizational levels. During gunnery competition among tank companies, do we send the best gunner to school as scheduled, or keep him in the unit to make a better composite gunnery score? Is the company commander in combat transplanted from the unit to attend a preordained school while the battle continues?

That "now versus future" contest is exemplified in the corporate world by highly visible quarterly profits competing with less conspicuous needs for research and infrastructure. Quarterly profits usually win. Leaders in all sectors have difficulty abandoning immediate rewards for the uncertain dividends of the future.

Another fundamental dilemma persistent in organizations is the contest between necessary centralized control that sets standards and coordinates operations, and the desirable decentralized mode that encourages local initiative. The natural tendency of organizational adjustment is a steady, often inconspicuous, flow toward centralization.

In a complex operational environment where only local initiative can adapt promptly to change, the bureaucratic tendency to control should defer to trust and decentralization. Denying a capable junior leader, the opportunity to exercise judgment is rarely the right option. More on this in Note 20.

At the strategic level, leading requires additional attention to building peer relationships with external entities—intra-governmental, joint, combined, or commercial. Also necessary is the capacity to build teams from mixed cultures, as with a Middle Eastern country or the State Department. Leading at that level includes exemplifying institutional values to both internal and external audiences. At best, it also includes staying within the unique responsibilities of the office, relinquishing meddling in tactical operations that is more fun.

At any level, a leader needs to review the job description and determine unique responsibilities. Bureaucratic job descriptions are often one-dimensional summaries designed to pacify the personnel office. They are usually inadequate, even as a starting point, in defining the essence of the task at the middle and senior leader level. In every leadership position, there are responsibilities whose neglect can compromise operations, inherent tasks neither boss nor subordinate can handle. Identifying and articulating them pays big dividends.

One obstacle in adapting to a new leadership role is the loss of emotional comfort sustained by mastered routines. It is tempting for a leader now in a higher position to prioritize based on previous responsibilities. While the small unit commander might worry correctly about which vehicle or how many are waiting for repair parts, the senior leader had better ignore which trucks are out of action and focus on production, shipping, and allocation of parts.

As leaders move to more complex roles, they will have staff and subordinates of considerable experience and maturity. A discerning, vigilant leader takes advantage of all available expertise and supporting systems. Listening is never a weakness.

Leaders set the example, articulate a clear mission, clarify priorities, provide a vision for the organization's future, safeguard prized traditions, build trust, support teamwork, develop subordinates, recognize and honor good work, build a supportive and challenging climate, represent the organization to external audiences, take prompt disciplinary action against those who violate ethical standards, and if needed rationalize sacrifice and keep hope alive.[3] Their vocabulary includes "I know you can do it!" and "Well done!' and "It was my fault," as well as "I don't know, but I'll find the answer." Leaders also understand they are critical cogs in the mechanism—key links between vision, people, and systems--but at no level the whole machine.

How we translate principles and good intentions into action—into routine behaviors and timely decisions—and then monitor organizational progress remains the heart of the matter.

The principles of strategy are simple. Their application is immensely difficult. Robert Strausz-Hupé[4] 1958

---

[3] Snider and Matthews, *The Future of the Army Profession*, 139-173. This definitive, comprehensive work spells out in detail the range of complex functions and responsibilities of Army leaders. It is essential reading for an informed discussion on contemporary professionalism.

[4] Robert Strausz-Hupé, 1903-2002, was a U.S. ambassador and a distinguished diplomat.

Principles of Leadership

Principles don't explain how to lead, but they have great value in articulating institutional expectations. Here are a couple of lists of principles plus my suggestion for a slight addition. (Lists of specific *behaviors* to be addressed later have considerably more utility.)

From a 1953 Publication

Command and Leadership for the Small Unit Leader was printed in 1953.[5] Its eleven principles of leadership attend to human aspirations. They are little affected by the gigantic technological and societal changes of the intervening sixty years. These principles still cover most of the bases. After each statement (in bold) are explanatory notes also taken from the February 1953 publication.

1. **Take responsibility for your actions.** … A willingness to accept responsibility is the foundation of all leadership … You give the orders of your superiors in your own name and with the authority of your office.
2. **Know yourself and seek self-improvement.** … If you are to understand and control others, you must first understand and control yourself.
3. **Set the example.** … No amount of instruction and no form of discipline has as great an effect on the unit's standards as your personal example.
4. **Seek responsibility and develop a sense of responsibility among subordinates.** … You should so discharge the assigned responsibilities for yourself and your unit that you can welcome an increase in responsibility.

---

[5] HQDA, *FM 22-100*. A primary leadership text at the time, it still provides essential information.

5. **Insure that the job is understood, supervised, and accomplished.** …Tell your subordinates what to do by issuing clear and concise orders. Through supervision, insure that your orders are understood and carried out.

6. **Know your men and look out for their welfare.** … Make a conscientious effort to become personally acquainted with your men… and you will have a better understanding of their capabilities and limitations.

7. **Keep your men informed.** … Make sure that your subordinates receive all the information necessary to do their job intelligently. In addition, inform them on matters having an indirect but vital effect on their initiative, enthusiasm, loyalty, and convictions.

8. **Train your men as a team.** … The duty of every leader includes the development of teamwork through the thorough training of his command, whether it be a squad, or an army group.

9. **Employ your command in accordance with its capabilities.** … Successful accomplishment of your unit's mission depends upon how well you know what it can and cannot do.

Example is the best general order. Major General George Crook[6]

---

[6] Major General George Crook, 1830-1890, was a noted leader in the Civil War and considered the Army's greatest Indian fighter. He developed a great respect for Indian culture and advocated for fair treatment of the Indian tribes.

10. **Make sound and timely decision.** ... If you delay or attempt to avoid making difficult decisions, you will not be able to make good use of your command.

11. **Know your job.** … This principle is, in effect, a summary of all the principles noted before.

I would add a number 12: Create a coherent and supportive organizational climate. (This would require application of the original eleven.)

From a 2012 Publication: The Mission Command Theme

Mission Command is a new title for old and powerful medicine difficult for hierarchical organizations to swallow: give clear guidance, provide resources, and give subordinates the encouragement and latitude to do the job. The eleven principles from 1953—especially if augmented by the proposed twelfth—should guide a successful implementation of the Mission Command philosophy. Its formal definition, from *ADRP 6-0*,[7] is "the exercise of authority and direction by the commander using mission orders to enable disciplined initiative with the intent to empower agile and adaptive commanders in their conduct of Unified Land Operations."

The reasons for persistent difficulty in putting that meaningful philosophy into routine practice are many. They derive from complex human ambitions within a profession critical in the life of the nation. Constrained resources and relatively unconstrained missions complicate the picture. Still, creating trusting, adaptable, and satisfying organizational climates that support Mission Command remains within the range of human skills, as evidenced by the high-performing units in the force. That creation is basically what this book is about.

---

[7] HQDA 2012. The latest effort to describe how leaders should make their intentions and orders clear and then avoid micromanagement while supporting subordinates in the execution.

Notes from the Notes of Part 1

PART 2

Professional Values and Command Philosophy

But, in case signals can neither be seen or perfectly understood, no captain can go very wrong if he places his ship alongside that of the enemy.

Horatio Nelson
at Trafalgar
October 21, 1805

Professional Values and Ethical Climates

Recently, our Army expended considerable intellectual energy in formally articulating the Army ethic—describing basic concepts of military professionalism that frame the culture. While some of that effort might have been well spent determining why traditional values are not always practiced, reviewing and articulating professional standards provides an essential baseline.

Back in the 1970s, Colonel Mike Malone summarized Army values in the four items listed below. Some current Army publications do not include *candor* in the list for some wrong reason. Importantly, in research extending from a 1970 study of officer behavior— the Army War College *Study on Military Professionalism*[8]—to a recent exploration of performance in Operation Iraqi Freedom (OIF) and the Afghanistan campaign Operation Enduring Freedom (OEF),[9] there was little ambiguity within the officer corps regarding professional values. There was also an intense concern by soldiers of all grades

---

[8] The study, directed by the Army Chief of Staff, responded to concerns about leadership climates in segments of the Army during the Vietnam era. It stimulated a variety of analyses and prompted review of personnel policies and leadership education. The bad news in the study (deviation from expectations for unselfish, competent leader performance) overshadowed the good (strong support for traditional values and deep concern when they were not upheld).

[9] USAWC, *Leadership Lessons at Division Command Level*, 2004 and 2010, contain data, assessments, and perceptions about their commanding general's leadership and the resulting organizational climates from immediate subordinates and staff officers in eight divisions, taken at home stations after return from a year in Iraq or Afghanistan.

when those values were compromised. The implementation and reinforcement of those values deserves our attention.

One Concise List of Institutional Values

Here is Mike's list— "Derived from sheer necessity on the battlefield"—along with some of his comments:

- **Candor** – Honesty plus openness … plus simplicity … The prime rule governing communications among soldiers on the battlefield. Candor develops and supports the trust upon which commitment is built.
- **Commitment** – A dedication to something bigger than self … to fellow soldiers, to the team or section or squad … to the larger units and the nation. Commitment is the foundation of coordination and interdependence. The ultimate in commitment is giving one's life in the service of others.
- **Courage** –The willingness to take a risk even when the choice not to do so is open. Courage is the catalyst of the battle: it grows in a unit from individual acts which generate trust and support commitment.
- **Competence** – Highly developed skills that are the basis of confidence, trust, and commitment. Competence undergirds all the other values of the battlefield. Competence plus commitment, courage, and candor means winning.

Leaders as Guardians of Professional Ethics

Placing others before self, perhaps the key professional ethic, remains a robust tradition in the American military. Reports from today's battlefields confirm that. Bold sacrifice is sufficiently commonplace to go unreported. Ethical behavior, along with mastery of essential skills, represents the heart of professionalism. It is prized because honesty and fairness are avenues to organizational effectiveness. Confidence that subordinates, superiors, and associates are ethical speeds up decision-making and breeds comfort. It is a hallmark of a healthy profession.

Professional values are routinely under siege by bureaucracy and unleavened human ambition. They must be nourished at every opportunity by every leader. These are essential leader behaviors for reinforcing the ethics of the profession.

- Explain and remind of the expected ethical behavior. Give specific examples.
- Ensure that senior leaders by word, deed, and policy exemplify standards.
- Fix any reward, competitive, or evaluative system that invites ethical ambiguity.
- Take prompt action against unethical behavior. This must be done even if it involves loyal friends from battles past—a formidable challenge for even the strongest.

A Report to Self on Ethical Corner-Cutting

Boldly scandalous behavior rarely damages traditional values. Spectacular transgressions are rejected outright by the community. Disregard for professionalism is not taken lightly in the body of the military institution. However, a potentially detrimental attack on professionalism can sneak aboard disguised as trivial, benign corner-cutting for "survival."

> Don't worry about the lieutenants. They will follow your example.
> Worry about your example.
> Walt Ulmer

The imaginary Form 1984[10] (Chart 1) offers an opportunity for organized reflection by self-recording an act of doubtful integrity. It might awaken perspective and discourage future deviation from ethical standards. Just discussing Form 1984 could be useful in a professional development session.

Chart 1. Report to Self on Cutting Ethical Corners

Report to Self After Cutting Ethical Corners:
a Value Priorities Awareness Exercise
Form 1984

Part 1. Event and contributing circumstances.

_____

Part 2. Why I took this action. (Check all that apply.)
- ☐ to protect the reputation of my unit
- ☐ to protect my boss or my subordinates
- ☐ to protect my career and allow me to continue to contribute
- ☐ to comply with pressure from my boss

Part 3. My excuse for deviating from my normal ethical behavior—and submitting a misleading/incomplete/dishonest/inaccurate report. (Check all that apply.)
- ☐ I just didn't have the time or resources to complete the requirement.
- ☐ The requirement was trivial and not worth completing to standard.
- ☐ I knew that my boss didn't care if I submitted a false report.
- ☐ By compromising a bit, my troops got a good deal. People know I'm honest.
- ☐ My boss is a good person, and I did not want him to get in trouble.
- ☐ An honest report might have spoiled my record. I want to get promoted and continue to serve.
- ☐ Everybody hands in false reports on this matter, and I have no reason to be different.

Part 4. What are my intentions about how to handle this in the future? Who will I discuss it with?

_____

_____

---

[10] This form--and all others in this book—may be reproduced for local non-commercial use. This book should be noted as the source.

Note

6

Loyalty, Can-Do, Fairness, and Collegiality in Perspective

Among the treasured behaviors that define our professionalism are loyalty, a can-do attitude, and fairness. *Loyalty* is the faithful response to obligations. *Can-do* is at the heart of a profession that places mission above individual welfare. The perception of *Fairness* in personal behavior and institutional policy is essential to a trusting environment. Although associated with the rise of democracy and meritocracy, even in ancient armies a leader's favoritism caused resentment. *Collegiality* is a pleasant residue from participation in a challenging environment alongside loyal associates.

Each of these noble elements of military professionalism has dysfunctional potential. A self-serving interpretation can rationalize mischief. Comprehensive leader development programs should include case studies of how these hallowed virtues have been manipulated to justify unprofessional behavior, as well as the more common reporting of how they have stimulated heroic performance.

When you are commanding ... your leadership will depend only to a minor degree on your tactical ability. It will be primarily determined by your character, your reputation, not much on courage—which will be accepted as a matter of course—but by the previous reputation you have established for fairness, for that high-minded patriotic purpose, for that quality of unswerving determination to carry through any military task assigned you. General George C. Marshall, Fort Benning OCS, September, 1941

Loyalty

The danger with loyalty in the raw is that multiple legitimate loyalties exist: to the boss, the troops, the unit, peers, the parent institution, the church, the family, the community, and—not unseemly—oneself.

Our military penchant for expecting individual efforts to be selfless seems a bit disconnected from reality. Few notable leaders have lacked ambition. *Unselfish* seems a more realistic aspiration. The boundaries of acceptable ambition are defined by what is seen as fair, ethical, and consistent with organizational goals. As long as career aspirations do not lead to manipulation that puts self above unit, peers, or subordinates, ambition is a beneficial—in fact essential—attribute.

Loyalty to the current boss versus loyalty to personal values and institutional needs is the most common dilemma. The pressure to make the boss or the unit look good by doctoring statistics—whether it be budget execution or micro payments to villagers or aircraft readiness or nonjudicial punishment—is easier to resist in theory than in practice. When the reporting system is itself suspect, the boss is well-liked, and our next efficiency report is pending, the harder right becomes harder. The correct path is rarely ambiguous.

Loyalty to a boss should not imply that subordinates must be intellectually captive team players, denying personal convictions to parrot the boss's view. A confident leader has no problem differentiating between disagreement and disloyalty. However, once the commander has made the decision there is no room for continuing dissent or even mild obstruction absent a clearly illegal or immoral order. Thoughtful leaders understand there will be conflicts among values and are prepared to make the choice for the "harder right"— in battle or in the conference room. The fundamental truth regarding competing loyalties is that "all animals are equal, but sometimes some animals are more equal than others."

Can-Do

The danger with can-do is that it can seemingly justify the imposition of "mission impossible." The resiliency, elasticity, and commitment that characterize military units can camouflage the damage done by persistent inadequacy of resources for the tasks at hand. For example, imagine a unit is given the impossible task of accounting for all serial-numbered items in twenty-four hours when that dispersed unit cannot even locate all the items in that time. Then the unit commander receiving the order has two options: explain to the boss that it cannot be done and deal with the boss's response, or submit a false report that all items were accounted for.

While such a clumsy order should never have been given—and the boss should not have passed it on if it came from higher—the fact is that a "take the hill at all costs" tradition can excuse managerial nonsense. The primary solution is for senior commanders to educate themselves about the capacity of their subordinate units (see Principle # 9 in Note 4), to listen to subordinate concerns about "missions impossible," and to ask the tough question, "Is my ambition subverting my decision-making?" For the subordinate, the only acceptable solution is to make every effort to comply with legal orders, to be straight with the boss on what is doable, and to never submit a phony report. Any other solution, no matter how temporarily comforting, portends trouble for self, organization, and profession.

Fairness

Fairness is critical to developing trust. But it can morph into convenient justification for policies that provide equal treatment or opportunity while placing the organization at risk. For example, the six-month command tour in Vietnam gave large numbers of lieutenant colonels a chance for battalion command, as well as a rest. But that policy raised hell with unit stability and cohesion. Also, it frustrated the competent and resilient battalion commanders who knew that six months in that environment was not long enough to best care for men or mission.

> Loyalty: The necessity for this basic military essential is so clear you scarcely hear it mentioned. Yet it is not automatic, and it is not always present—up, down, and laterally in equal degree—as it must be. General M.B. Ridgway

Fortunately, we learned to be more attentive to operational needs during OIF and OEF, although early on some company commanders were sent home against their wishes to attend school while their units remained in combat. The fashionable desire to be incontrovertibly fair to individuals who have conspicuously misbehaved by insisting on exploring all conceivable avenues for their defense can represent fairness run amok.

Perfect fairness is an unwieldy tool in peace, and can be an institutional banality in war. Mutual trust and discipline can suffer when focus on fairness becomes unfair to the organization.

Collegiality

The list of noble but occasionally abused values within the profession includes collegiality. Collegiality is a refreshing form of esprit de corps or social cohesion that makes life in a profession more enjoyable in good times and more resilient in bad. But that same collegiality can be anathema to monitoring and enforcing standards. Records of every war reveal both strong friendships and petty disputes at work in forming or undermining teams. The final order of battle may be born as much from friendship as from assessed competence for the task at hand. (For classic examples in World War II, see Mark Perry's *Partners in Command* and James Scott Wheeler's *Jacob L. Devers.*) The troop lists going into Desert Storm and Iraq were formed as much from compatibility of three-and four-star personalities as from comparative unit suitability.

> Haunted by that spirit of camaraderie which, in the army, has done us so much harm, certain high officials hesitated to apply the red-hot iron where it was most needed. General Jean Mordacq,[11] 1920

---

[11] General Jean Mordacq, 1868–1943, served in the Foreign Legion in Indochina, was twice wounded in 1817–18, and as a captain had been saber champion in the French Army. He was recognized for scholarly writings and for innovations in military schooling.

Peer reviews do not have a history of success as guardians of institutional values. This is particularly true in a society where friendships born of mutual sacrifice are strong and enduring. Giving a failing grade to a subordinate unit for its physical security deficiencies is one thing. Reporting a fellow officer for making a false statement requires courage of a different order.

The articulated expectation is that adherence to institutional values will trump personal friendship. Leaders must reinforce at every opportunity the primitive concept that "a soldier on guard has no friends." Leaders must also make clear the rules of the game, with no "missions impossible" that could be used to rationalize cutting ethical corners.

Circumstances and Values Prioritization

Conscious value prioritization in anticipation of a possible ethical dilemma is a counterintuitive exercise. But it can build ethical muscle and preclude ethical crises. This prioritization applies both to personal behavior (such as playing favorites with individuals) and to organizational decisions (such as playing favorites with units). Leaders need sensitivity to potential ethical side effects as their decisions make their way down the chain of command. Competent leaders craft decisions that do not create ethical dilemmas for their staff or their subordinates.

In a squad versus squad competition in an obstacle course race we have a clear obligation to be fair to all competitors. That would include all teams having the same starting time, etc. In a tactical situation where we need the best scout platoon to take the lead on a dangerous mission, we may unfairly send the least-rested but best-led platoon because it has the greatest chance of success. We can be legitimately unfair as we focus on the bigger picture.

At every level, leaders need be alert for policies that have potential for sacrificing effectiveness under the guise of ensuring fairness. Consideration of fairness to women, for example, regardless of how such assignment opportunities might or might not enhance organizational effectiveness, represents understandably emotional competition between legitimate—if institutionally unequal—values. Fairness to crucial organizational goals can be more complicated in an environment rightly sensitive to social issues.

If I am to be hanged for it, I cannot accuse a man who I believe has meant well, and whose error was one of judgment and not of intention. Wellington, 1809

Note

7

A Personal Philosophy of Leadership

A personal philosophy is not designed for any particular place and time. It is an expansive template for taking command of self. Thinking through and recording how we intend to lead and serve can be remarkably productive. As with strategic planning, the process is often worth more than the product. You may have heard some of these pithy statements of a personal philosophy. They are catchy but need further work as useful guides to behavior.

> "My philosophy is simple: get good people, tell them what needs to be done, and then let them alone!"

> "My philosophy can be stated very simply: treat others—boss, peer, and subordinate—just as you want to be treated! Make the world better!"

> "I can spell out my philosophy in a very few words: demand loyalty, reward excellence, and punish failure!"

> "My philosophy is to set high standards, exemplify those standards, clarify goals and priorities, provide resources, give feedback, praise in public, and correct in private!"

> "My real philosophy is to take charge, and do whatever is necessary to win!"

An Outline for Recording a Personal Philosophy of Leadership

1. What is the primary purpose of leadership in my life? (What do leaders do that makes me want to be one?)

2. How do I evaluate my success as a leader? (Who and what will determine my success as a leader?)

3. How do I earn the trust of subordinates, peers, and bosses? (What steps will I take to earn trust?)

4. How do I express my appropriate trust of others? (What kind of decisions and behaviors will send the right message?)

5. How do I control and monitor the activities in my organization without micromanagement? (What methods will I use to clarify policies, gather information, and establish control and coordination without denying subordinates appropriate freedom of action?)

6. How do I communicate within and outside of my group or organization? (How will I keep individuals, my staff, other organizations, the public, and any other stakeholders informed? What kind of items will I keep only to myself or a trusted few? How can I best use and control high-tech devices and systems for personal and group communication?)

7. How do I involve others in the decision-making process? (What criteria will I use in deciding how and when to include others? How will I encourage that practice in my organization?)

8. How do I coach subordinates and assess their performance? (What obligations do I have as a coach? How do I get to know the interests and aspirations as well as the aptitudes and attitudes of my subordinates?)

9. How do I maintain some kind of balance in life, given competing loyalties to self, family, community, organization, and profession? (Is balance a meaningful concept? Do we really mean instead a rationally organized life? How is such

balance reflected in focus, priorities, schedules, assignments, expectations, and personal example?)

10. How do I protect, not squander, the authority of my position as a leader? (How will I exercise both the formal power and moral authority of my position? How will I avoid abuse of power? How will I avoid failing to take decisive action when necessary?)

11. How do I use the special courtesies and privileges afforded an organizational leader? (What courtesies and trappings do I need, if any, to signify my role as leader? How will I avoid abusing the privileges of my position? How will I support and respect and stature of subordinate leaders?)

12. How will I continue to learn and grow as a leader? (What are my plans for informal and formal continuing education? How can I get reliable feedback about my behavior? How do I prepare myself to listen carefully to legitimate feedback? Can I find a true mentor?)

An interesting exercise is to rewrite from scratch, for your own review, a philosophy of leadership—or of life—about every five years. This is a productive, nonintrusive, inexpensive component of continuing self-education. It is not unlike rereading Durant's *The Lessons of History*[12] (short version!) or, in the military genre, *Once an Eagle*[13] every year or two.

> Enlightened leadership is service. The leader grows more and lasts longer by placing the well-being of all above the well-being of self alone.
> Lao-tzu. Sixth century BC.

---

[12] *The Lessons of History* by Will and Ariel Durant is a distillation of a life's work reflecting the essence of human nature and the societal structures and challenges that emerge.

[13] *Once an Eagle* by Anton Myrer is an exciting historical novel and a military classic that captures the essence of the American military tradition and the struggle between personal aggrandizement and unselfish service.

Note

8

A Command Philosophy

Some organizations require a written philosophy, or broad intention of performance, from leaders when they assume command. The purpose is to stimulate thinking on how one intends to exercise authority and achieve goals. Here are two examples.

The first example was mine as a corps commander. We at corps headquarters elaborated on that philosophy and supporting policies in a booklet about leading, training, maintaining, and fighting. That "Green Book" had many suggestions but few demands. It was designed to clarify philosophy and policy without undercutting the authority or initiative of subordinate commanders. It received good reviews.

All organizations need clear mission guidelines and operational standards, just as they need latitude in mission execution. Assembly of nuclear/chemical rounds, the position of attention, PT and gunnery standards—these do not permit local interpretation. The degree of accurate compliance with specific standards is a legitimate test of organizational discipline, revealing whether orders can move reliably and coherently down the chain.

Philosophy is broad stuff, painting the big picture and providing a rational and ethical basis for acting. Perhaps composing the philosophy is the most productive part of the exercise. It should stimulate reflection on how organizations can and should work. Like strategic plans, a command philosophy deserves discussion and feedback to ensure its understanding and relevance. Left unattended—rarely affirmed, contested, or revised—such a philosophy does little harm but little good.

A Command Philosophy Written in 1982 for a Corps

"The process of building fighting units requires more leadership than management, but smart management is also essential. Recognizing that we have responsibilities for both immediate readiness and the future vitality of our Army, we must build motivation, confidence, and mutual trust within our units—even in the face of horrendous personnel turbulence. The most productive expenditure of a commander's time is that devoted to explaining the mission, defining subordinate responsibilities, and clarifying standards. (Many subordinates remain reluctant to ask for the clarification they sorely need.)

If we are sure that a subordinate understands the responsibilities of the mission, both immediate and long range; if priorities are understood; and if the subordinate is honest, our management strategy should be heavy on trust and latitude and light on intrusion and control. That tactic has a prime chance to build a sense of individual responsibility for outcomes. The major contribution of a senior headquarters toward building a healthy and productive climate at unit level is to provide a coherent, predictable, and non-hectic environment within which the unit commander has the time and energy to be a leader. Effective, innovative training and maintaining are mostly the products of individual motivation and cannot be sustained through rigid managerial techniques.

Every system has a finite amount of managerial energy. It can be expended in two ways: protective reaction or innovative excursion. If commanders expend energy looking over their shoulders, preparing defenses against inspections or judgments from above, and building a statistical fortress, there will be minimal energy left to coach and innovate. (More on organizational energy in Note 33.)

Every organization has two sets of priorities. One is the commander's articulated priorities, such as "get the troops in good physical shape." The other is operational or all de facto priorities, such as "all mechanics to the motor pool at first light." The goal is to synchronize the implementation of programs and priorities so there is no conflict between the two to generate frustration or rationalize unethical behavior.

Because "discipline is the soul of an army," we pay attention to faithful response to orders. True discipline is self-discipline. However, exercise of the chain of command in providing clear instructions and enforcing compliance with traditional artifacts (precise drills, clean weapons, meticulous uniforms, etc.) is essential in building a team and forming habits.

A Command Philosophy from Company Level in the 1980s

This crisp, direct memo reflects enlightened integration of "managerial" and "motivational" concepts. It reeks of common sense. The author indirectly addresses many of the conceptual issues faced by all organizational leaders while also touching on daily activities found at the bottom of hierarchical organizations.

The officer who produced this guidance had a notably successful command tour. Perhaps the philosophy described here contributed to that success. I wish I had written something like it for one of my company commands. Here are excerpts.

> **"Introduction**: Most good units have developed for themselves a consistent way of doing things to cut down on confusion and wasted time. Normally this is called standard operating procedures or SOP. It is not totally restrictive and allows for and encourages subordinate decisions … It is for all soldiers in Bravo Troop.

> A. Admin and Personnel
> ✓ If a subordinate soldier asks you a question, it is an important question … answer it, find out the answer and get back with him, or train him to find the answer himself.

He who continues the attack wins. General U. S. Grant

34

- ✓ Soldiers are our most important asset. If you don't believe this, find a new job.

- ✓ My open-door policy is as follows: any soldier can talk with me about anything, anytime, anywhere. I encourage the use of chain-of-command, but there's some things that some guys just gotta talk to the ol' man about personally. Please respect this, and don't ever let me catch you giving a soldier hell for using the open-door policy.

- ✓ If there is an alert, you have let too many soldiers go on leave/pass, and you can't fight the enemy … report to PAC [personnel office] with a 4187. Check the block labeled "Request for reassignment." I'll sign off.

- ✓ If you are a good, honest, hard-working soldier, you will get promoted. Hang in there and have good faith.

- ✓ No graffiti. The Army has given us a nice barracks for our soldiers to live in. The Army has also given us shelter halves [for individual tents] to live in if we can't keep the writing off the walls.

- ✓ Encourage "Sure-Pay." Then train subordinates how to manage a checkbook.

- ✓ Treat new guys nicely. They feel the same way you felt when you were new. Remember?

- ✓ If you use drugs and think it makes you witty, the joke is on you. Please stop and/or leave this unit before we catch and embarrass you. Same goes for alcohol.

- ✓ A soldier who has a happy family life is usually a better soldier … Soldiers and their families are in Bravo Troop … We spend a lot of time in the field, so we need to give them the best quality time when we're at home.

B. Supply and Maintenance

- ✓ We are not *using* the Army's equipment … we *own* it.
- ✓ Don't sign for anything you can't put your hand on.

✓ Say "thanks" to the support guys once in a while. They do a lot of work and we take a lot of the credit.

C. Training

✓ When you train for one thing, don't forget the others.

✓ Everything we do is training. It is up to us to make it worthwhile.

✓ I like to put things out in formation because then I know everybody gets the word "straight from the horse's mouth." But when I do, I'm not being a very good trainer.

✓ The difference between a good NCO and a bad NCO is that the good NCO will find reasons to train; a bad NCO will find excuses not to.

✓ Maintenance is training.

✓ Border duty is training in disguise.

✓ Some things are training, some things are tests. Get to know the difference between the two. There can be training without a test (but there shouldn't be), but there is no such thing as a test without training.

✓ If it's stupid or dumb, take a second look at it before you do it.

✓ Do everything in your power to make training fun.

D. Leadership and Discipline

✓ In order to be a good leader, you must be a good follower.

✓ If a lot of your soldiers are going over your head to get answers, you're doing something wrong.

✓ Good leaders are not immune from getting their hands dirty. Lead by example!

✓ Rules about mistakes:

✓ a. Mistakes are authorized, but not encouraged.

✓ b. Don't make the same mistake twice.

✓ c. Have the courage to say "I made a mistake!"

✓ Lead to impress your peers and subordinates. Don't spend all of your time trying to impress your superiors. Have faith: they can tell a good soldier from a bad one.

✓ Discipline is not for the bad soldier. It is for the good soldier, to protect him from the bad soldier.

✓ There is no such thing as an "acting" anything. If your PLT SGT is on leave and you are taking his place, you are not the "acting" PLT SGT; you *are* the PLT SGT.

✓ Leadership is presence. Either the PLT LDR or the PLT SGT will be with the platoon at all times. NO exceptions! Soldiers expect this and I demand it.

✓ There is a difference between "cutting slack" and "looking the other way." Learn the difference.

✓ At all costs, fight the urge to overreact. A good leader is calm, cool, and collected."

Note

9

Measuring Leader Success

There are practical reasons for exploring the parameters of success. Rational, ambitious, confident, capable individuals are well served by defining what success means. Our metrics for personal success or whatever we label comfort with the outcome of our work and relationships make a difference. They draft aspirations and expectations for our future, draw boundaries for our behavior, and influence our passion for the task at hand.

Successful may be the least precise word in our vocabulary. Its definition remains elusive after two thousand years of deliberation. It might mean "satisfaction with my contribution" or "comfortable with my level of promotion" or "keeping all my promises" or "winning all my battles" or some combination thereof.

Where do the reliable judges of success reside—the analytical but emotionally complex self or the historically crafted, institutional record? Meaningful criteria for success ought to reflect both personal and career expectations. Formulating a workable definition may be particularly difficult for professionals in an institution driven by honorable effort and mission success. In addition to wanting to lead "a good life," "be a leader with integrity," "care for my family," and "be true to my faith," specific career goals rise up:

> A clergyman, or a doctor, or a lawyer feels himself no whit disgraced
> if he leaves the end of his worldly labors without special note or honor.
> But to a soldier or sailor such indifference to his merit is wormwood. It
> is the bane of the profession. Nine men out of ten who go into it must
> live discontented and die disappointed. Anthony Trollope,[14] 1858

---

[14] Anthony Trollope, 1815–1882, was a respected and prolific English novelist with a wide range of interests.

- graduate from Ranger School
- get a master's degree
- attend the Command and General Staff College
- command a battalion
- be a positive link between military and civilian worlds
- become Chairman of the Joint Chiefs of Staff
- contribute to the development of strategic doctrine
- develop personnel systems that attract and retain high quality people

Determining Success Within the Institution

Aspiring leaders may enhance their chance for career success by completing every mission on time, on budget, with minimum casualties; motivating team members to do their very best; coaching subordinates so they can be better leaders; having the best materiel readiness rates in the organization; or building a reputation for innovation. How well any good work (or bad) is noticed and faithfully entered on the ledgers of the institution remains a critical part of success—if success consists primarily of formal institutional recognition and promotion.

The most reliable measure of our success as leaders is the product of our work. Probably the best available method is to assess the quality of the organizational climate we have developed. Almost as reliable as measures are the frequency and significance of our victories in battle. The *almost* is because enemy, weather, and inadequate firepower can be insurmountable obstacles; and not all leaders have the chance to lead and triumph in battle.

Generating a high-quality climate is less dependent on unpredictable, independent variables. Individuals and organizations increasingly appear comfortable with both the methods and the outcomes of climate assessments.

Considering methods as well as outcomes in the leader evaluation process is not a new invention. Generals in earlier wars have been fired because of "low troop morale" or "draconian methods" regardless of their battlefield victories. The rising expectations for wide opportunity and protection from institutional abuse are also contributing to the increased attention on *how* a leader gets results.

In modern societies, there are fewer sanctuaries into which the king can retreat and avoid scrutiny. That reality, along with advances in the behavioral sciences and various technologies, has facilitated intrusion into individual and organizational privacy. For current organizational leaders, this adds familiarity with methodologies for assessing individual and organizational productivity to their tool kit. (Notes in Parts 5 and 6 relate to this issue.)

Great Captains and Successful Captains

A history of great captains may be the wrong place to find neat answers, but the conspicuous ups and downs of historical figures offer some insight about concepts of success. Some well-known characters whose actions changed history demonstrate the difficulty of defining success by some universal criteria. "Successful" military leaders often win their battles—but not always. Grant, Lee, Rommel, Alexander, and Napoleon had bad days when a lot of people died without capturing the hill. Robert E. Lee and Erwin Rommel, respected by their soldiers and tactically competent, remain notable—if newly controversial-- military leaders despite losing critical battles or, as in Rommel's case, serving a despicable regime. Obviously, effort, skill, and win-loss record all count, as do perceptions of overall character and contributions to civilization.

Successful military leaders must be of high moral character—or maybe not always. Great captains like Nelson and Wellington took flagrant liberties with social norms. Should one who saves the empire be given a bit of latitude regarding off-duty behavior? Is there such a thing as "off duty" in a community of professional practice? While blatant disregard of societal expectations for proper behavior may impair a leader's moral authority, the criteria for moral rectitude seem somewhat elastic. The institution needs to clarify the limits of good behavior.

Success and Ethical Behavior

Measures of success often overlap and interact. As with values, there must be a conscious attempt to create some kind of hierarchy of values, prioritizing one feature of success over another. Unfortunately for the added complexity it brings to the party, context plays a role.

Much leadership in war or peace takes place in arenas less physically threatening than an evening stroll down the back streets of big cities. Perhaps only half the individuals deployed to war zones ever hear an incoming round. But whether in combat or classroom, one aspect of success depends on how well we navigate ethically hazardous waters.

Ethical strength may be stunningly clear to those present at the moment—the leader "took the heat" when he could have passed the buck downward or "put her career on the line" by introducing contentious data at the meeting. At the other end of the spectrum, perhaps the leader identified a subordinate as the responsible party when in fact the failure was his own. But capturing for the record reliable assessments of routine ethical behavior absent spectacular dishonesty remains a challenge. Professions generally do not have laudable records in assessing, recording, or policing it. Peer reviews are notoriously feeble links in the chain of ethical accountability. Leaders at all levels should be active in identifying potential or ongoing ethical malpractice and be diligent in its exposure and in examining its source.

Success, the Halo Effect, and Reality

We know that leaders who are conspicuously successful in tactical battle are not automatically suited for higher command. Still, the military institution understandably prizes tactical acumen in battle so highly that the resulting halo effect can contaminate the process of selecting leaders who will be successful also in high positions.

Moving up the ladder we recognize that different effectiveness criteria come into play. Tact, patience, high cognitive ability, and sensitivity to context become powerful players. These characteristics are only moderately developable by institutional intervention.

Clearly all outstanding leaders cannot be successful if reaching the top rung of the hierarchy is the sole objective. In practice, success must come to grips with legitimate expectations. And systems for selection for promotion do not always get it right.

Of the four most outstanding colonels I worked for, each revered by subordinates and peers, only one was promoted to general officer. Meanwhile, one brilliant but known to all subordinates as a highly toxic colonel made it to lieutenant general before being exposed.

Interestingly, the percentage of general officers disappointed with their careers upon retirement may be higher than that among retiring lieutenant colonels. I have no empirical data on this, but am pretty sure my conclusion is correct. It has something to do with ambition, self-image, ego, and need to continue contributing. It also has something to do with the relatively small number of positions at the top of the hierarchy and the situation (good for the institution) that more individuals are qualified than top slots available.

Never give an order that can't be obeyed. General Douglas MacArthur

There needs to be, within our ethical compass a juggernaut metric that outranks others. That would be the unfailing belief that doing the "right thing" ultimately counts most. Leaders can help the institution and organization in this arena by keeping ambition in perspective. They can help also by coaching their subordinates on the complex and potent topic of how to define success. Success and failure have two judges: self and the rest of humanity. Failure may be more easily determined and commonly affirmed, with self and others more likely to agree.

It is amazing what you can accomplish if you do not care who gets the credit.
President Harry S. Truman

Notes from the Notes of Part 2

PART 3

Critical Leader Behaviors

Your position never gives you the right to command. It only imposes on you the duty to so live your life that others may receive your orders without being humiliated.

Dag Hammarskjöld

Note

10

Behaviors That Can Lead to Success

This list makes sense to a wide variety of audiences. Its components are also common in the behavioral science literature. (I have used it in discussions from graduate school to grade school and they all seem to get it—at least in theory!) It includes one critical assumption: for these behaviors to ensure success, the leader must first make sound and timely decisions.

I call this short list the big four. These behaviors set the stage for success in any scenario and in perception from any direction—downward, upward, and across. As discussed in the preceding note, resources and environment preclude any set of behaviors from guaranteeing outcomes, and a satisfactory universal definition of success remains elusive. Given all that, the odds of both short- and long-term mission accomplishment as well as personal satisfaction are greatly enhanced by these four ingredients in the recipe. Their routine practice would surely result in awarding any boss an *A* for effort.

- **Set the example**. Represent in your routine behavior the values you preach.
- **Explain** what you want individuals and organizations to do—and why. Do it often. Confirm you are understood. Do not let your directives or intent become lost or distorted in transmission to the user.

- **Listen** to others. Clearly welcome experience, suggestions, and feedback.
- **Be fair** in all your dealings. Never play favorites with individuals or units.[15]

Although their relative importance may differ between training and combat, key behaviors are quite independent of context. Also, how we lead in combat is greatly determined by habits formed in the months and years beforehand. The new variable in the combat setting is physical fear and, in some settings, the speed of required decision-making under stress.

Only a small percentage of our leaders flunk the physical courage test. In the American experience when that occurs there are fortunately other leaders or subordinates who jump in to quickly fill the gap. That jumping in is rare in armies with no democratic history.

Controlled stressful training can provide some degree of protection against any panic under fire that could immobilize a leader. Well-led, high-morale organizations that score well in rigorous training typically produce wins in battle.

Individual characteristics that enable behaviors

In order to routinely exemplify the four behaviors, individuals must have certain characteristics or capabilities. Some of those seem dependent on genetics, confirmed or amplified by supportive experiences in the very early years of life. Some capabilities enabling desired leader behavior are amenable to development through education, training, and experiential learning.

> The art of leading, in operations large or small, is the art of dealing with humanity, on working diligently on behalf of men, of being sympathetic with them, but equally of insisting they make a square facing of their own problems.
> S. L. A. Marshall in *Men Against Fire*[16]

---

[15] Bekoff, Wild Justice. It seems more than interesting that some animal species have strong feelings about fairness, as well as tendencies toward empathy and cooperation. Fair play is an extraordinarily powerful human need.

[16] Marshall, *Men Against Fire*, 160. There have been disputes of some of the quantitative data in Marshall's writings, but this book rightfully retains a spot among memorable discourses on small unit leadership.

The following capabilities are particularly important for leadership in the complex environment of the twenty-first century. However, their development and honing is mostly beyond the scope of these notes, where we focus on behaviors that derive from these characteristics:

- **Cognitive power.** This ability to observe, discern, and decide is relatively immune from substantial enhancement by any known reliable process. It is also the most important. It greatly determines the ability to make sound decisions on time. The level of required intellectual competence—understanding that "intellectual competence" comes in various forms—obviously depends on the complexity of the decision-making environment. It can depend also to some degree on the presence or absence of other capabilities.

- **Need to be engaged.** This result of seemingly complex internal drives is expressed in a "take charge" attitude and a willingness to take risks to create change. It is facilitated by self-confidence which is also somewhat genetically based.

- **Capacity for clarity of expression.** This is based substantially on cognitive power but is affected considerably by learned habits of speech, self-control, and insight into the needs of the audience—an aspect of empathy. It may be the characteristic most susceptible to enhancement by training and example.

- **Energy level.** Effective leadership demands emotional and physical stamina in a variety of scenarios. It can be enhanced or diminished by lifestyle, but seems to be considerably determined by genetics.

- **Empathy.** Understanding the needs and views of others is important at all organizational levels but becomes increasingly critical for senior leaders. It is an enabler for enhancing teamwork—for crafting policies that recognize different needs and expectations among team members. It is difficult to self-assess.

- **The capability to trust and delegate.** Dealing effectively with complexity and ambiguity requires the leader to empower subordinates and employ their expertise. This attribute also may be linked also to "hard wiring," but experience and cultural immersion play a role in its development.

- **Emotional resilience.** Leaders must be able to keep cool under stress, bounce back from disappointment, and carry on when things look bad and it's raining. The jury is out on our ability to significantly modify resilience, although feedback from stressful training regimens and a dose of enhanced self-awareness can provide some degree of immunization to panic and some relief from emotional overload. I am not greatly hopeful about major constitutional reconstruction absent a pharmacological or neurological breakthrough.

Differences Between Tactical (or Direct) and Strategic Leadership

The need for continuing education of senior leaders in order to keep abreast of nuances of global politics, technological breakthroughs, and the special demands of management of large complex organizations remains clear. Further, there is probably merit to education exposing potential senior leaders to the complexities of strategic and intra-governmental operations, as is done in the senior service colleges of our armed forces.

However, the idea that a wholesale revision of basic leader behaviors is needed to make a successful transition from tactical to strategic has been overblown. The fundamental differences between tactical and strategic decision-making derive from difference in scope and complexity. Implementing strategic decisions effectively requires the capacity to delegate and an understanding of information pathways and barriers in complex organizations.

The competencies in these areas are crafted significantly by genetically induced tendencies. Undoubtedly, they can be nourished and honed by formal education, mentoring, and experiential opportunities. To gain the most advantage from experience, we need to form a model for reviewing past success and failures, take time to discern contributing factors, and plan how best to apply new insights.

Today an abundant variety of education sources are convenient, no longer limited to the classroom or senior officers' tutoring. Global updates are at the fingertips of anyone interested. If the result of this convenience in absorbing strategic precepts is in doubt, convene a small group of company or battalion commanders. You will find among them sophisticated strategic thinking and an awareness of most of the issues with which top leaders are wrestling. There is no longer an enclave of strategic thinking available only to the upper echelon. The trick, then, is to locate and motivate the many junior officers who have innate ability and desire to join the ranks of strategic leaders, and to appreciate their awareness of strategic matters.

There is also a need for awareness that behaviors that might have worked well in junior years can lead to failure at higher levels. There have been multiple studies concluding that if hard-charging, impatient, aggressive junior leaders do not upgrade their interpersonal skills—in particular, listening and empathy—any career at the strategic level might be brief.[17] Strategic leaders fail most often because of inability to form and sustain relationships; or for insensitivity to context; or for misbehavior that would also get a lieutenant fired.[18]

Lessons Captured Vividly from Life at Sea

Compelling notions about leadership are often recounted well in tales of the sea. It may be easier to visualize the captain of a ship on the high seas than a commander of a ground unit in the jungle. Ship's captains are often depicted at the extreme: the despised and ruthless or the revered and respected, Bligh and Queeg or Nelson and Jones. There is

---

[17] McCall et. al., *The Lessons of Experience*. This notable CCL product remains relevant. Since 1988, the components of "derailment" have not changed appreciably. Technical competence is rarely the heart of executive failure. It typically results from poor interpersonal skills, neglect of context, or integrity issues.

[18] Jacobs, "A Guide to the Strategic Leader Inventory." This document, prepared for students and faculty, outlines concepts, individual competencies, and performance requirements for strategic leadership.

nothing more exciting or informative about leadership than the Patrick O'Brian Aubrey-Maturin tales of high adventure at sea in the early nineteenth century![19]

In 1939, the U.S. Naval Institute thought it time for a booklet on leadership to be used at the U.S. Naval Academy. It gathered ideas from a variety of experienced officers, most but not all of them naval. The booklet was titled *Naval Leadership with Some Hints to Junior Officers and Others*.[20] Its first item was, "A Letter from John Paul Jones to the Naval Committee of Congress, 14 September, 1775." Here are extracts from the 1939 fourth edition:

> It is by no means enough that an officer of the navy should be a capable mariner. He must be that of course, but also a great deal more ...
>
> Coming now to the naval officer aboard ship and in relation to those under his command, he should be the soul of tact, patience, justice, firmness, and charity. No meritorious act of a subordinate should escape his attention or be left to pass without its reward, even if the reward be only one word of approval. Conversely, he should not be blind to a single fault in any subordinate, though at the same time he should be quick and unfailing to distinguish error from malice, thoughtlessness from incompetency, and well-meant short-comings from heedless or stupid blunder. As he should be universal and impartial in his rewards and approval of merit, so should he be judicial and unbending in his punishment or reproof of misconduct.

---

[19] O'Brian, Aubrey-Maturin series. This series, starting with *Master and Commander*, may be the best combination of exciting sea stories and the essence of organizational leadership ever written. The books reek with wisdom.

[20] United States Naval Institute 1939, xv. Way prior to WWII, the Navy sensed a need for a convenient handbook to assist in officer leadership education. This short booklet was the very impressive result. It was used early at the Naval Academy. Copies are hard to come by but remain in Navy archives.

In his intercourse with subordinates he should ever maintain the attitude of a commander, but that need by no means prevent him from the amenities of cordiality or the cultivation of good cheer within proper limits. Every commanding officer should hold with his subordinates such relation as will make them constantly anxious to receive an invitation to sit at his mess table, and his bearing toward them should be such as to encourage them to express their opinions to him with freedom and to ask his views without reserve."

Who could say it any better in 2017? With technology since 1775, big changes. With people, not so much.

Once Upon a Time, Long, Long Ago …

… our team and a few thousand South Vietnamese soldiers were surrounded by a substantial contingent of the North Vietnamese Army. That had been the case for a few weeks, and it was to go on for a few more. We had in our organization experience and teamwork and, everything considered, high morale. There was magnificent support from the U.S. Air Force, the U.S. Navy, and a bunch of great Army aviators.

Outside the perimeter was a target-rich environment. Often two or three USAF forward air controllers were busy at the same time. For one ten-day high-intensity period, they averaged about 260 strikes per day around the town. Some air support came from aircraft carriers cruising far away.

When the carrier-based aircraft arrived overhead, sometimes with low fuel, a target was needed in short order. Normally not a problem, since we had targets aplenty. One morning when a flight of four showed up, however, there was nothing at the moment that grabbed our attention as a candidate for five-hundred-pound hard bombs.

A few days earlier, a helicopter driven by a determined crew that avoided anti-aircraft fire and miscellaneous other hazards had brought us new call signs, mail, rations … and a couple packets of M&Ms, a real treat. One red M&M dropped from my hand onto the 1:50,000 map sheet used for targeting. It landed on a spot about one kilometer outside the perimeter where there had been some movement days before.

So, with the approval of the Vietnamese division commander who had quickly checked the map to see if there could be any farmers still in that area, we gave the FAC the coordinates of a "suspected enemy location" at the spot where the M&M hit the map.

At that moment, everybody in the command bunker had the same information. We trusted each other's competence; there was no time to make an environmental impact assessment or have a group discussion about alternatives. I told the FAC, "Hit it!" And the fast-movers did. Then the FAC described erupting from the strike point the biggest explosion and cloud of black smoke he had seen in a long time. We had hit an enemy ammo dump.

The FAC and the U.S. Navy pilots were impressed. "You guys down there are real pros! Don't know how you do that stuff!"

"No problem," I said. "All in a day's work." It was simply pure luck, although our prompt decision-making did facilitate the good fortune.

Years later, in a room full of staff experts discussing the redesign of corps-level communications architecture, another kind of decision was required. The one-man show suitable during battle now had no place in decision-making. There were captains and senior civilians present in the large conference room who had forgotten more than I knew about the technicalities of preventing electronic spectrum overlap and so on. There was time for deliberation. I did have preferences about how part of the design would affect ease of communication with adjacent headquarters, among other things.

The operable question here is whether or not we can adjust our behavior to context. Can we move from a prized, comfortable tactical mind-set to a more thoughtful collaborative mode? What in our culture encourages sensitivity to context? What in our system rewards such adaptation?

Encouraging adaptation to environment represents a challenge to a culture understandably biased toward today's observable results over tomorrow's ambiguous possibilities. But neither do we want, nor could the institution tolerate, a dysfunctional practice too common in hierarchical organizations of leaders in any context avoiding decisions when decisions are required.

Note

11

Behaviors That May Lead to Disaster

Describing disaster is easier than defining accomplishment. Measuring its behavioral components seems handier, more universal, and less dependent on context. Fortunately, dissecting the corpus of a failure has become commonplace in many organizations.

The U.S. Army's after-action review (AAR) process is a shining example of an institutionalized procedure for candid review and analysis before the heat of the moment wears off.[21] Tactical matters—the taking of a village, the construction of a bridge, the laying of a minefield—are more convenient targets for immediate analysis than the less evident components of decision-making at the administrative or strategic process. This is particularly true at higher organizational levels where a variety of transient cooks may be in the kitchen.

But all decisions are framed and made by people. In a structured review process, certain behaviors will stand out as major contributors to outcomes. Analyses of decision-making where large staffs play a major role in supporting senior executives can be particularly productive—even if rare. The reality is that it is too often a review is left to post-war historians. Questions of such variety as why the subordinate never received a warning order, why the horses ended up on a different ship from the wagons, why the

---

[21] HQDA 1993. The now-accepted protocol of all-ranks open discussion of the good and bad elements of an operation and their likely cause shortly after its completion has become a healthy standard procedure in many units. Most often used after tactical operations, it has enormous potential in analyses of administrative operations.

order that 80 percent of the truck fleet must be operational when there were not enough repair parts in the known universe to keep them running, why the covey of colonels needed to cluster in the Pentagon hallway to agree on what the general wanted done, and why the major training exercise had been planned to start on the Monday after Easter can be traced to the following "big six" that portend disaster:

- routinely putting personal agenda above that of the organization
- making promises and not doing your best to deliver—or not explaining why you can't
- showing moral or physical cowardice when under pressure (moral is the tougher issue)
- never telling anybody or any organization what you really want them to do
- being insensitive to the views and aspirations of others
- making poor decisions on time or perfect decisions too late

Unproductive Behaviors Prompted by Information Technology

New technologies and devices have proven enormously helpful for improving the dissemination of information, collecting data, exchanging viewpoints, and issuing instructions. However, if not consciously and properly managed, phones, tablets, and pads can slowly depersonalize relationships, absorb great chunks of time, complicate staffing processes, and spread immature information over a wide area. They can become addictive as well as disruptive.

Here are a few practices to watch for in our high-tech era—behaviors of seemingly benign impact that can undermine leader effectiveness:

- spending increasing time with electronics and less time with people
- staying behind the computer too long and getting outside the tent too little
- counseling by e-mail or remote video

> It is better to act quickly and err than to hesitate until
> the time for action is past. Clausewitz, 1832

- becoming swamped with mountains of unrefined data
- letting indiscriminate, spectacular, unfiltered information interfere
- allowing unrefined, unstaffed information to be released
- overwhelming subordinates or staffs with trivial requests by pushing a button
- over-watching by drone and interfering from afar
- demanding perfection in graphics whose creation absorbs enormous energy
- responding prematurely to all information in sight
- checking e-mail and other graphics while being briefed or in discussion
- not ensuring that classified or sensitive information is kept in proper channels
- not providing clear guidelines for the general use of personal communication devices in both tactical and administrative situations
- converting the work day to a 24-hour exercise by unlimited after-hour texting

Once Upon a Time, Long, Long Ago …

… most company-sized units had their own mess hall—no consolidated, impersonal dining facilities. In A Company, our mess hall was not doing too well. Inspectors found rodents had made a home in the cupboard; the griddle did not pass the temperature test for frying eggs; and the cook's "whites" were a sort of mottled gray. Also, unbeknownst to the inspecting team, our mess sergeant had a fondness for strong drink during the day. Most important, the food was not good. Our troopers deserved better.

The missing ingredient was leadership. The mess sergeant did not have enough. We put in a requisition for a new mess sergeant (I say "we," but I was a second lieutenant platoon leader with the additional duty as mess officer and also acting executive officer), assuming the folks up at squadron headquarters would agree that the current situation was untenable, meals were not up to cavalry tradition, etc., it would be weeks or months before we had a replacement.

We had a platoon sergeant who was a model leader. He knew weapons and tactics. His troops stood straight and hit their targets. He was a square-jawed picture of a professional NCO. He was a leader, and we needed leadership in the mess hall. So, while we waited for an official replacement, we made him the mess sergeant.

He noted that he was in totally new territory, was not pleased with his new opportunity, but accepted the task. He really had no choice. We mentioned it should not be more than a couple months before a new mess sergeant would arrive. Then he could return to his platoon.

He immediately took action. Soon the mice were gone from the storeroom. The cook's whites became closer to white. The food got no better, but it was usually served on time. Then a notable incident occurred that reinforced a basic point: inspirational leadership cannot compensate for lack of technical skill.

Every Tuesday, each mess sergeant filled out a requisition for items that would be delivered the following week from the central warehouse. Apparently, we were out of bay leaves. How many bay leaves did we need? None of the cooks were sure except that we were out. Our temporary mess sergeant took a guess. He ordered twenty pounds.

Ever thought about what twenty pounds of bay leaves looks like? Well, they fill a good portion of a semi-trailer. The next weekly delivery to our mess hall included stacks of bay-leaf-filled cardboard boxes about four feet high and six feet wide. (All but one box was returned the following week.) We absolved our acting mess sergeant of his clerical error, but when a slightly overweight but experienced mess sergeant reported in a few weeks later, our relief was monumental.

From that incident, which I recall as if it were yesterday, the following two lessons emerged:

1. Inspirational, dedicated people without relevant skills are rarely the solution.
2. People in warehouses (and in other parts of the infrastructure) do not always apply the commonsense rule: if it seems really dumb, check it out before you execute!

Note 12

Two Recent Studies of Leader Behavior

Studies of the leadership styles of a sample of division commanders who led in Iraq and Afghanistan confirmed once again that behaviors for which Chamberlain, Grant, Wellington, Washington, and other heroic commanders were admired still produce results. Both the 2010 study *Leadership Lessons at Division Command Level—2010: A Review of Division Commander Leader Behaviors and Organizational Climates in Selected Army Divisions after Nine Years of War* and its 2004 predecessor[22] found that subordinates in an active theater put these at the top of the list of desirable behaviors of their leaders:

- can make tough, sound decisions on time
- sees the big picture; provides context and perspective
- gets out of the headquarters and visits the troops
- keeps cool under pressure
- clearly explains missions, standards, and priorities

The primary survey instrument used in this study, shown in Appendix A as the Leader Behavior Preferences Worksheet, was developed from Army doctrine; related research and studies; and the experience of the study team. After drafting, it was vetted in several Army units to ensure relevance and clarity. Again, surveys such as this articulate institutional values and priorities, and advertise command interest. If not compromised

---

[22] USAWC 2004 and 2011. The 2004 study was replicated in four other divisions for the 2010 version. Conclusions were generally the same, with a slight decline in the quality of climates in 2010.

by clumsy administration, they can contribute to the development and sustainment of a healthy climate.

The survey protocol included a small group discussion immediately after survey completion. Those discussions provided background and rationale for the responses to the various items. Anonymity was guaranteed to both individuals and organizations. Typical discussions were informal, candid, and greatly assisted the study team in formulating conclusions.

Making Decisions on Time

At one vetting session with a group of captains prior to commencing the survey, the draft had included "Can make tough decisions on time." All of our items were framed in the positive direction, and a response of "strong agreement" would reflect good leadership.

One officer raised his hand and said, "My battalion commander makes tough decisions all the time. But most of them are wrong!"

We changed the item (number 22 on the instrument shown in Appendix A) before using the survey to "Can make tough, *sound* decisions on time."

If we did the study again, I would revise that item further. It would be, "Can make tough, sound decisions *and ensure they get to subordinate leaders* on time." We found that in many cases, the commander made a timely decision as soon as he had appropriate details of the situation. However, a major component of the delay was passing the decision through the staff and down intervening organizational layers to the ultimate user.

An extensive study of CEO behavior reported in 2017 highlighted the importance of timely decisions.[23] One of the conclusions from this survey of over 17,000 executives was

---

[23] Botelo, et. al., "What Sets Successful CEOs Apart," from the robust CEO Genome Project, also confirmed once again that interviews were not a reliable method for selecting senior executives. They reveal little about decision-making or keeping cool but do provide clues to cognitive and verbal ability.

that "deciding with speed and conviction" was a far better road to success than a lengthy routine of meticulous exploration of mountains of data looking for a perfect solution.

Keeping Cool Under Pressure

"Keeps cool under pressure" is characteristic of every successful combat leader. It is relevant also in a stressful meeting in an air-conditioned room. The salient question is how do we train people to keep cool? My sense is the capacity for resilience and calmness under duress is about 80 percent nature and 20 percent nurture. The behavioral science literature tends to be heavier on the nurture side, but it may be coming around. The *nurture* part comes mostly from observing others who set the example by keeping calm, and by stressful training with prompt feedback from on-site observers—such as at our National Training Centers. Again, it seems possible to inoculate to some degree against panic, understanding that modifying any aspect of emotional resiliency is no small chore.

In attempting to screen candidates for stress tolerance that would facilitate keeping cool, there is merit in well-managed procedures designed to challenge and stress the candidate both mentally and physically. While at times past bordering on sophomoric hazing, the stressful treatment of new cadets at West Point may have been reasonably effective in rejecting those whose emotional resilience was questionable.

Yes, there will be some unfairness in any early screening process. A few potential Churchills may be rejected. Overall, the emerging cohort will be more robust without those who cannot withstand combined emotional and physical stress. In screening for potential leaders early in any profession, identifying the unfit is more important than identifying potential top performers. There will be time later on for that.

The first qualification of a general is keeping a cool head ... He must not allow himself to be elated by good news, or depressed by bad. Napoleon, 1831

Our special operations organizations have used challenging exercises for screening and developing with considerable success. In the process, they have been careful to avoid demeaning or shaming, and have assured candidates that failure from one program does not imply failure in the entire profession

There is pride in surviving the rigors of intensive screening. Few soldiers in the modern era have complained that their initial training was too hard, the discipline too intense, the standards too high. While some of that may be fashionable macho response, it is too commonplace to disregard. We spurn traditional rites of passage at our peril. In any case, keeping cool deserves mention in both selection and development. Emotional fitness screening for all potential military leaders may need to be more comprehensive and intense than is the current norm.

Future introductory military training might need to be further subdivided: tougher for combat arms, less physically grueling for those whose battles will be mostly in conference rooms where key decisions are born. Since success or failure for leaders is determined more often by ethical and cognitive than physical fitness, those more complex and often politically sensitive domains deserve continuing review for potential innovation.

Good Leaders with Behaviors Still to Work On

It was noteworthy that the nine division commanders involved in the 2004 and 2010 studies generally received high marks for overall leadership. The "system" had produced a number of major generals whose job performance was seen by the most intimate observers as commendable. Several commanders were viewed as truly outstanding, if still imperfect.

In surveys over the years at level from platoon to corps, the most prized behaviors stood out across a variety of environments. However, how good leaders can improve were also conspicuous. The following specifics were identified by subordinates in the 2004 and 2010 studies.[24] These, again, are group results. The items do not apply to all the division commanders who were studied but were common enough to warrant mention.

The following are items in order of importance as deserving more attention as seen by subordinates:

1. Adapts quickly to new situations and requirements.
2. Keeps cool under pressure.
3. Knows how and when to involve others in decision-making.
4. Clearly explains missions, standards, and priorities.
5. Sees the big picture; provides context and perspective.
6. Encourages initiative and welcomes new ideas.
7. Gets out of the headquarters and visits the troops.
8. Coaches and gives useful feedback to subordinates.
9. Sets a high ethical tone; demands honest reporting.
10. Can make tough, sound decisions on time.
11. Senses unproductive policies and makes prompt adjustments.
12. Holds people accountable for their actions and results.

The survey with its entire twenty-nine items is in Appendix A.

Typical Descriptive Quotes from Lieutenant Colonels and Colonels

Following is a sample of written comments about their division commander, an opportunity provided on the survey form. These comments are from brigade commanders, deputy commanders, battalion commanders, and key members of the division headquarters. Comments such as these—some provided in writing on the survey form and some from informal discussions immediately after the surveys were completed—were used

---

[24] USAWC 2010.

to explain and confirm the quantitative data. They were provided anonymously within the study protocol.

Naturally, survey team credibility and performance have considerable impact on the candor of participants and the validity of conclusions. Surveys and discussions were with small groups usually ranging from four to six individuals of the same grade (all lieutenant colonels or all colonels with the formal survey, with larger groups of captains for an informal survey of company commanders). General officers and division chiefs of staff were normally surveyed individually. These interviews usually took place from a few days to a couple of weeks after returning to home station from typically yearlong deployments to Iraq or Afghanistan. These complex environments provided considerable stress and challenge for leaders at all levels.

The following were positive quotes (the vast majority of anonymous comments about the eight participating commanding generals were positive):

- "He talks to soldiers and listens to commanders."
- "He admitted mistakes."
- "He is a team builder. He did not play favorites."
- "He was coaching us how to listen."
- "He was thoughtful, unpretentious, pragmatic, approachable, and big picture."
- "He was around a lot, but not just to catch something that was wrong."
- "He was highly intelligent, common sense, and down to earth. Low maintenance."
- "A big change from the former CG. We went from directive to supportive."
- "He was brave to the point of subordinates' concern for his safety."
- "He listens even if he is not entirely comfortable with the message."
- "He demands ethical behavior and honest reporting."
- "It's hard to select his shortcomings. He is remarkably good."

The following quotes described what the commanding general "needs to work on":

- "We waited a long time for some decisions. We needed answers."

- "His relations were better with his commanders than with his staff."
- "He was approachable, but not often accessible."
- "The CG was open, but sometimes the staff confused the situation."
- "It took his HQ a long time to identify poor policies and promptly change them."
- "He was initially unsure about how to employ my unit. But he listened and learned."
- "Too much staff direction. Let me know the intent and we will get it done."
- "I didn't get coached as much as I wanted, but with his schedule he did his best."

Exploring Levels of Subordinate "Closeness" to the Division Commander

One finding that emanated more from discussions than analysis was the importance of perceived differences in the quality of relationships between the division commander and various immediate subordinates. Fairness—or in this particular setting, the apparent differences in access that portrays one aspect of fairness—is surely a consequential behavior.

In the few cases where perceptions of favoritism on the part of a division commander came to light, it was painful for the outliers. This was particularly true if that division commander was highly regarded for his competence and commitment—somebody likely to go places.

When a senior commander's behavior says his favorite is the commander of the fires brigade, or it appears he has a mind meld with the intelligence officer, or he shares family secrets only with the chief of logistics, it fuels uneasiness. Whether or not apparent closeness results in preferential treatment, it still poses a challenge to a sense of fair play. Senior executives are often unaware how their personal relationships with different team members can impact the climate. The question is how to explore this delicate issue with the individuals involved while "doing no harm."

The Leader Relationship Map (LRM)

A senior member of our study team—an experienced retired officer steeped in the world of executive selection and education—suggested an innovative method of capturing and comparing the perceived closeness of relationships between the top commander and immediate staff and commanders. This could reveal perceived dysfunctional cliques or reflect a normal distribution of varying degrees of closeness as expected by role or frequency of association.

The Leader Relationships Map created by Colonel (Retired) Mike Shaler was used a few times in the 2004 and 2010 studies. Its potential for exacerbating nervousness about any existing feelings of favoritism is apparent. But its unique utility merits its consideration as part of a complete review of senior officer team-building.

To administer that instrument, we used with what we titled the Predicted Results Comparison (PRC) model.[25] Each participant indicated how close he felt to the division commander and also offered observations on how close the other participants were. Comparison of the data was invariably interesting.

A decision on who gets to see what parts of the data needs to be agreed to early in the process. Ideas of how the boss sees different levels of closeness in relationships and how subordinates see these relationships is a methodology probably best restricted to an emotionally mature audience. The exercise facilitator must have a delicate hand. Results can be especially helpful to a truly gifted leader who needs—and can accept—a nudge to modify and enhance behavior. Strong, generally competent leaders are not automatically team-builders.

The Utilization of Field Research Like These Studies

The degree of persistent institutional follow-up to the 2004 and 2010 leader behavior studies is unclear. Among the many leadership studies ongoing at the time, these were

---

[25] Use of the PRC is further described in Appendix A, items 2 (APDO) and 3 (ACC.)

taken seriously by those in charge at the moment and referenced in officer education programs. Efficient use of sponsored research remains a challenge for any institution.

Research findings in all busy organizations, unless taken under the wing of an interested senior leader, quickly embedded in institutional doctrine, or saved by spectacular headlines, die a fairly prompt death. Nevertheless, thoughtful pulse checks of leaders and organizations are increasingly essential for any institution to satisfy both internal conscience and supporting public.

Once Upon a Time, Long, Long Ago …

… we created a peer rating process in a training center whose purpose was to convert volunteers into soldiers through eight-weeks of heavy indoctrination, training, and education. We aimed to produce soldiers with the dedication and skills needed to complete their tour of enlistment with excellence. We designed a brief form to capture trainee perceptions that might bring additional insight about performance and potential to that gleaned from the close daily observations of experienced drill sergeants.

We went about this somewhat crudely, probably violating whatever rules on survey participation were in vogue at the time (over forty years ago). In any case it proved useful. At the end of the second and fifth weeks, each trainee would complete the form in pencil. We would review the results and ask the drill sergeants if there were surprises.

Notable but not surprising was that after just two weeks of stressful training amid close living there was consensus among trainees on which of the forty members of their small groups were seen as best and worst characters. These results changed very little from the second to the fifth week of training. The characteristics that displayed high or low potential for future military service were quickly apparent to peers. The drill sergeants were not surprised at who were identified as the best potential soldiers. But there was considerable surprise about some who were near-unanimously identified as poor soldiers by their peers but had been given passing marks by the cadre.

My guess was that two key ingredients of a good soldier were more conspicuous to peers in the after-hours barracks and encampments than in the classrooms or combat pits or rifle ranges under the eyes of the instructors. These two ingredients were unselfishness and cooperativeness.

It now occurs to me that flagrantly selfish behavior, apparent early to peers in a situation demanding shared workloads, might reveal a toxic personality. But I am not qualified to make that judgment. We do know that peer ratings in a training environment—as used liberally in Ranger and Special Forces training among others—have high potential for detecting leader-relevant characteristics. Greater use of early selection out of the institution based on psychometric instruments and peer and staff observations seems warranted.

To implement widely such protocols—now restricted to elite formations-- we need an institutional commitment to force quality that can withstand the criticism of inevitable mistakes. We will indeed throw some good babies out with the bathwater. But there will be fewer remaining who have the potential for ultimately contaminating their units. In the big picture, fairness to the institution should prevail. Entering our Armed Forces is a privilege not a right.

Here is the response (Chart 2) by a trainee after his second week of basic. His identification of the best soldiers was mirrored by the responses of his platoon-mates. Agreement among peers identifying who would *not* make good soldiers was even higher.

Chart 2. Peer Evaluation of Trainees

Peer Evaluation of Trainees (Week 2)

A. Within your squad which two members do you think will make the best soldiers?

Ans: 1. *Tim King 2. Joe Jack*

B. Within your platoon which two members will make the best soldiers?

Ans: 1. *Tim King 2. Fred Smith*

C. Are there any in your squad or platoon who will not make good soldiers?

Ans: *Yes.*

D. If you answered "yes," please write their names down.

Ans: *I do not know their names. I don't even like to be around them.*

Other comments? *(He did not make any.)*

DO NOT SIGN YOUR NAME. *(He did not!)*

Note
13

Mentoring, Coaching, and Counseling

Mentoring, coaching, and counseling are essential for enhancing skills and perpetuating traditions. They play a primary role in the mix of institutional efforts to develop leaders, complementing formal education and local instruction. The three terms are ill-defined and overlapping, a reality that can limit their potential. This is in spite of a multitude of web-based explanations attempting clarification.

Mentoring

Mentoring can be a powerful tool for passing on both skills and the essence of institutional culture. Current Army doctrine describes it as a "voluntary developmental relationship." *Voluntary* is important. Some institutions demand leaders have mentors, and assign mentors without consulting the mentee. But mentoring effectiveness, as with all one-on-one adult learning, depends considerably on the emotional as well as the cognitive or institutional relationship.

In true mentoring, each of the parties must be interested and comfortable. Mentoring can blossom into long-term friendship while providing a stimulating transfer of knowledge and perspective. Before commencing the formal process, there should be agreement on the rules of the game: what subject matter will be the prime target, how often and by what means mentoring sessions will take place, and how value-added will be measured.

The current boss is a poor choice for formal mentor: too close to daily operations, difficult to detach from the inherent evaluator role, and normally too busy to attend to

70

mentoring needs of several subordinates. Additionally, while a productive mentoring relationship might last many years, most bosses stay in place for a relatively short time. However, if the boss is a natural teacher and the subordinate a determined learner, informal mentoring and coaching could take place and also continue pleasantly past the immediate boss-subordinate assignment.

Mentoring, interestingly, remains a contentious concept, sometimes a pejorative term interpreted as a notable senior managing a protégé's career. We hear of World War II generals having mentors who contributed greatly to their development. A closer look at some cases reveals that some of the advertised "development" was considerably the mentor bypassing the system and facilitating assignments. It is an interesting cultural evolution within the institution that the notion of an influential sponsor paving the way for somebody is seen increasingly as inappropriate.

The perception of advocacy or hints of cronyism too often triggered by the word *mentoring* can inhibit the healthy transfer of the wisdom of experienced individuals. Perhaps a new term is needed to better describe the function. A title like "institutional tutor" might do the trick. In any case, studies indicate that officers who have had true mentors—not simply advocates-- are more satisfied with their careers than their peers who have not had a mentoring experience. As with all teaching, the teacher also learns— sometimes more than the student.

Coaching

Coaching is the least confusing of these terms. The role of a coach in American culture is widely understood. Sports giants still have coaches. A coach provides guidance designed to improve performance. Leaders at all levels need to coach—and to learn how to give constructive feedback that includes objective commentary on both methods and results.

Studies continue to indicate that subordinates in every kind of organization rarely feel they are receiving constructive behavioral feedback on a regular basis. In fact, our Army is probably ahead of the pack in meeting this need, but the pack seems well behind the needs of the day. Members of our society expect individualized attention and constructive advice.

In thirty-three years of active duty, I received two sessions of unhurried performance feedback: once as an assistant battalion S-3 of an amphibious tank and tractor battalion, and once as an assistant professor in the department of earth, space, and graphic sciences (renamed long ago) at West Point. Over the years, there were some ad hoc meetings with bosses when something was commended, and several after I had screwed up. Those brief sessions normally focused on a single event, not on the pattern of my behavior that had contributed to the success or failure. I recall also cursory mentions of strengths and weaknesses at the moment that the boss laid my efficiency report on the table: the least appropriate moment for receiving feedback, most learning neurons being disabled at that time.

Counseling

Counseling has been so long associated with "ass chewing" that the word has lost much of its meaning as a tool for constructive feedback. It might still deserve a spot in our dictionary, however, since professional feedback on a range of topics—from drug and alcohol to financial planning—come under its title. Recently there has been an upsurge in mandatory counseling sessions for the junior ranks. Where these sessions are preceded by instruction in how to tackle the task and are not burdened by paperwork and reporting, they appear worthwhile. Unfortunately, they can morph easily into ticket-punching exercises where the only organizational outcome is a report on who showed up on time. Often such mandatory sessions do not last past the tour of the local commander who was rightly taken with the concept that sessions of performance feedback are worthwhile and warrant guaranteed execution.

A properly designed survey instrument (the items make sense, and it is not too long), administered competently (its potential is explained, and the rules about who sees the results are clear), that provides feedback on specific behaviors has enormous potential.

The 360 approach where individuals can compare perceptions of their behavior with those of the boss, peers, and subordinates, is the most reliable method of gaining precious insight that permits us to improve as leaders. The 360 process can be part of mentoring, coaching, or counseling.

Receiving and Giving Feedback

Both giving and receiving feedback require study and practice—hopefully with a coach. When done right, the feedback process consumes considerable individual and institutional energy. It is also a function that can be rationalized as something to do "tomorrow." The basics are easy to understand, a bit more difficult to apply.[26] In giving feedback:

- By your attitude, make the feedback process as comfortable as possible.
- Provide an introduction that includes what you are attempting to do, the rules on confidentiality, and what if any follow-up there will be.
- Explain how you obtained the data that formulated the feedback content and your assessment of its reliability.
- Explain why the topics being discussed are important.
- Focus on what happened, not why you think it happened.
- Do your best to make the feedback session separate from an evaluation session.
- Explain what resources are available for follow-up.
- If there is a facilitator present, ask that the role be explained.
- Leave time for questions.

In receiving feedback, make the following your goals:

---

[26] Chappelow, "360-Degree Feedback," in the *CCL Handbook of Leader Development*, 58–84. A good background for understanding this process that is in increasing use in our military as a contributor to leader development.

- By your attitude, make the feedback process as comfortable as possible.
- If the feedback giver does not explain the rules and expectations, ask that it be done, particularly regarding confidentiality and final resting place of the data.
- If there is a facilitator present, ask that the role be explained.
- Do your best to listen carefully, take notes, and wait a bit before defending yourself against any apparent bad news.
- Save any question or doubts about the validity of the data for the end of the session.
- Don't hesitate to ask the feedback giver to explain any comments that you do not understand.
- Ask what resources are available for follow-up.
- Ask if there will be an opportunity to discuss the data after you have had time to review and evaluate it more thoroughly.

Any feedback is only marginally effective if it is not reinforced on the job. That finding has been confirmed in research time and time again. For feedback to make a lasting difference, the boss must participate regularly in the individual's development. That is done by the boss first showing interest, then routinely coaching and assisting in the effort to measure progress toward developmental goals.

The 360 process is a time-consuming but uniquely effective intervention. Recent efforts to require such interventions along with structured feedback have high potential as steps forward. Still, if poorly administered, without careful handling of individual data, and without explanation of their part in the overall personnel system, such interventions can be energy-eaters and trust-busters.[27] Some beneficial behavioral changes can be accomplished by less rigorous methods.

---

[27] Victoria Guthrie and Sara N. King, "Feedback-Intensive Programs" in the *CCL Handbook of Leader Development*, 25–57. There may be more here than the typical leader needs to know about various aspects of developmental feedback and related topics, but it is a convenient introduction to relevant conceptual aspects.

Once upon a time, not too long ago…

… I held for a year the General of the Army Omar N. Bradley Chair of Strategic Leadership, jointly hosted by the U.S. Army War College and Dickinson College, neighbors in Carlisle, Pennsylvania. I taught a one-semester elective at both institutions. In a few of the class sessions we combined Dickenson students with the Army War College students who were about the age of the Dickenson students' parents. That dynamic worked unsurprisingly well in reminding that good leadership looked remarkably similar to college juniors and experienced military officers once they compared and discussed specifics. But this brief story is about the lively classes at Dickenson College.

Dickenson is a first-rate institution with high standards campus-wide. In those days as I fear now, student speech was often filled with elements particularly disconcerting to those of us more chronologically gifted. It seemed that even the potential Phi Beta candidates in the classroom could inject "Like you know" into most spoken sentences. So, at mid-first day of class I mentioned that their speech might be more impressive in class and after graduation if they were willing to limit such phrases in some venues. I added that it would certainly give me joy if that happened during out sessions. We worked together (obviously not with equal status since I was grading their papers!) to follow a technique sometime seen at construction projects to track accidents. We put on the blackboard a sign that said "This class has gone _____ days without a 'Like you know!'"

Believe it or not, we had very few bursts of "Like you know" from then on. There was no need to add numbers to our prominent score-keeping chart. As a matter of fact, late in the semester when one young man used the phrase, we all pretended not to hear so as not to embarrass him about violating the new norm. Habits had been changed, at least temporarily, by a combination of accepting a potentially beneficial rule, an evolving peer pressure—albeit subtle--to conform, and continued observable interest and monitoring by the leader. It is basically the pattern we use to modify behavior, perhaps with more emphasis on compliance, in formal organizations. While it may take years of behavioral counseling, if ever, to change our hard-wiring, adjusting many behaviors is within the grasp of most leaders if there is a clear and sustained mutual effort and somebody keeping score.

Perpetual optimism is a force multiplier. General Colin Powell

Senior Leaders as Teachers: A Wish Is Not a Command

Good leaders are teachers. They teach at every opportunity. Senior leaders have experience to share—especially if they kept notes. But typical boss-subordinate relationships do not encourage the informal flow of ideas needed between teacher and student. The more complex the subject matter, the more essential the opportunity for comfortable discourse. Teaching the prone position in marksmanship is relatively independent of instructor–student rapport. Explaining the advantages and limitations of empowering subordinates requires a different level of understanding between teacher and student.

Seniors set the stage and make room for teaching and learning. They must by word and manner make clear the difference between a comment and a directive; between a lecture and a conversation. The idea that a general's wish is a command is nonsense. With the right climate, senior officers can ruminate, explore, and even prescribe without confusing the troops. A commander can be decisive and still open to disagreement. Subordinates in a healthy climate can differentiate between teaching and directing.

Units with respected leaders and strong discipline are normally the most open to candid discussion and loyal disagreement. Weak leaders often see disagreement as disloyalty, are sensitive to questions that might imply criticism, and can be upset by suggestions. With such a leader, it is even more critical—if uncomfortable or even hazardous—to prompt a discussion about separating suggestions from commands.

In reinforcing the difference between suggestions and directives, a senior could host a discussion of subordinate leaders' favorite ideas about topics of immediate interest. For example, how best to cope with a shortage of training ammunition, or limit the visitors from Washington, or get company commanders away from their laptops. An assembled group of company or battalion commanders might explain ideas on accounting for weapons or tracking the result of micro loans to local merchants or switching platoon leaders for a month or whatever. There would be a prohibition against verbal acceptance or rejection of any particular idea. The final comment from the host commander might be: "Thanks for explaining your ideas. Use any of them you want. I have made no decisions about their becoming mandatory or proscribed. If and when I do, I will make that clear." Creation of a teaching/coaching environment probably enhances a leader's capacity to have his orders carried out with dispatch when given.

I cannot leave this issue without mentioning two instances where I made casual remarks that created really dumb policy that only months later did I fix. The culprit was me. I had believed erroneously that our policy of "If it's dumb, it's not our policy!" was in full effect. I assumed that even in the heat of operations, somebody would confront me with any apparent dumbness before executing.

Once Upon a Time, Long, Long Ago …

… at a staff briefing during a division-on-division maneuver in Germany, I mentioned that some of our five-ton trucks had underinflated tires. Maybe, I suggested, we should do some tire-pressure checking before we had an accident. Since tire-pressure gauges were in mechanics' toolsets and on-vehicle kits but not otherwise handy, I suggested we buy a few and spread them around so leaders could spot-check tire pressure when appropriate.

About three months later—on a cold, muddy, hungry early morning on the tank gunnery range—a lieutenant walked over to me after his platoon finished a pretty good run and said, "General, can I ask a question?"

"Sure," I replied.

"I don't understand your policy on tire-gauges."

I replied, "What policy is that?"

He said, "That all platoon leaders in the division have to carry a tire-gauge at all times. General, I don't have tires. I just got tanks!"

So, we had to have another meeting at division headquarters.

The fundamental question was why, after a year in command, my "don't do it if it's dumb" policy had not permeated throughout our culture. Why for three months did nobody down the chain complain to me about the dumb order?

Several years later, I was lecturing at the Army War College. I had included that tire-gauge story in my talk. At the break, a student who had been a lieutenant in our Division Materiel Management Center at the time of the tire gauge incident confessed that his group was the source of the dumb tire-gauge policy. Wanting to help, they had sent an information bulletin through technical channels about my concern for tire pressure.

About three years afterward, still not having learned my lesson, I mentioned to an assistant post engineer as we walked through ongoing construction that I hoped all the new buildings would not be white. Again, I thought that our policy about dumb stuff had permeated through all parts of the community. Not so. A few weeks later, a wife who lived up the street mentioned that the post engineer shop no longer offered small cans of white paint to quarters occupants so they could touch up the woodwork. In fact, the word was out that a new post engineer policy was "no more white painting anywhere." This was hard to believe. We had to have another meeting!

Note

15

Trusting the Leader

Mutual trust within an organization is the glue that holds it together, the lubricant that minimizes friction, and the catalyst that encourages empowerment. It has enormous impact. Trust comes in two varieties: between individuals (leaders, followers, peers) and between individuals and the parent institution ("I know I'll get a fair deal in this outfit" or "The system will screw you every time"). The former is the subject of this note, the latter of the next note. For optimum productivity, both kinds of trust must be in effect and reciprocal.

The list of behaviors below, describing trusted leaders, comes from personal experience, research, and discussions over many years. Many audiences contributed to its formulation. Some were military, some civilian. Across time and venue, their suggestions for inclusion in the list were dramatically similar. The items on the list are consistent with Note 10's behaviors that lead to success and with our findings in the division commander studies outlined in Note 12.

A trusted leader:

1. Makes sound, tough decisions on time (and delivers them promptly to the operating unit)
2. Keeps promises; has "integrity"
3. Explains missions and priorities
4. Trusts others; does not routinely micromanage

5. Does not play favorites

6. Remains calm under pressure; can handle "bad news"

7. Shares risks, dangers, and hardship (risks to the flesh were not a concern; risks to the career were!)

8. Backs up subordinates; takes heat if needed (the rather commonly perceived need to shield subordinates by "taking the "heat" instead of passing it on deserves attention itself as a cultural matter)

9. Is predictable and consistent ("predictable" is more important than "consistent")

10. Keeps confidences (the issue is not about "classified" material but with personal information)

11. Places mission and unit above career

The eleven "trusted leader" behaviors are in order of importance from the collective perceptions of subordinates. The list could have included additional items, but these eleven stood out dramatically from others. Subordinates remain the best judges of leader performance in areas of encouragement, motivation, fairness, honesty, and unselfishness.

The top six items are in order based on most-often mentioned and also in my judgment most important. The ranking is from an amalgamation of informal input. The remaining five items are not in any particular order. Observations about relative importance as trust-building behaviors varied depending on the audience. Item 10, for example, on keeping confidences, seemed more important to civilian than to military groups; meanwhile, item 7 on sharing hardship, was more important to the military.

The relative priority among these eleven could vary. A field or administrative setting might elevate one behavior or decrease another's importance. Further, solid performance in one behavior might lead to less concern that the leader is a bit weak in another. If, for example, the leader, come rain or shine, "makes sound, tough decisions on time," some failings in other areas might be excused. In fact, almost any leader misstep can be tolerated if decisions inevitably lead to efficient mission accomplishment. Still, if decision-making were perfect but the only strength it would not guarantee sustained satisfaction with leadership.

No doubt at all about the power of the top three items on the list. Making sound decisions, by the way, is more managerial than motivational. Keeping promises would be more motivational. Segregating these items into any leadership-versus-management categories would not greatly illuminate the discussion, but does remind of the necessity for competence in both motivational and managerial domains.

The capacity to "trust others," allows the leader to be a legitimate candidate for being seen as trustworthy and thereby capable of empowering subordinates. Of course, trusting without accompanying essential behaviors and insights cannot generate respect or confidence.

I hesitated for years to add "Keeps confidences" to the list. But it was suggested so frequently in group discussions that I now include it, with the understanding that it has nothing to do with classified material, only with personal information. In the current environment, where written assessments like 360-degree feedback data abound, I can better appreciate the concerns that led to its inclusion.

I was also reluctant to include "Predictable and consistent," since there is nothing worse than a predictably consistently bad leader. It is also true that predictability and consistency greatly relieve subordinate stress. Relevant allied questions are how leaders acquire these behaviors and how the institution explains, evaluates, reinforces, and rewards them.

Small Examples of Trust-Building

The fundamental method for building trust is to routinely exhibit the eleven listed behaviors. There are a few particular techniques that senior leaders can use to help the process. As part of both subordinate education and climate-building, orchestrated interaction between seniors and juniors remains useful. This does require senior leader time and effort. While ultimately worthwhile, sponsors of such efforts must have a kind of cathedral mentality—knowing objective results of efforts may not be apparent during their tour in command.

In all earnest efforts to open communication and build trust, the notion that "familiarity breeds contempt" is nonsense. That is, unless the senior leader has been using hierarchical isolation to hide contemptuous behavior.

Another example of enhancing trust between subordinates and "the system" and senior leaders involves exposing junior leaders to the decision-making process at higher headquarters. (This can also lead also to confirming their worst fears!) Inviting a few company officers to a division staff briefing to see what the staff folks have to contend with can be an eye-opener. How the staff presents the commander with data and alternatives, how the group processes information, how senior officers listen, and how in touch higher staff officers are with ground reality can enlarge perspectives. Comparing multiple perspectives of any event, particularly of staff processes, can be a learning experience.

Trust might be reinforced by inviting junior leaders, say company commanders, to join the brigade or division commander at a meal or for a beer at day's end—if beer is still an acceptable beverage.

"'Tony, I don't know you, but the Army has made you a battalion commander, so you have my unwavering trust …' In five sentences, Col MacFarland had displayed more combat leadership than I had experienced … in Desert Storm, or … during the previous six months." Lieutenant Colonel Tony Deane, 2006[28]

---

[28] Deane, *Ramadi Unclassified*, 148. This is a notable work by a perceptive and dedicated commander. It reveals the complexity of contemporary operations and the thoughtful and innovative leadership that commanders are providing.

After-hours gatherings remain the pleasant norm in many organizations. We closed some of our officers' clubs to save a few dollars without giving thought to the magnitude of loss in team-building opportunities. It's kind of like cutting the number of military bandsmen who provide a traditionally inspiring function with broad impact that projects well beyond their numbers.

Saving a few manpower spaces made a small dent in size of the overall force, but crippled much military music. Both decisions are indirect products of an under-resourced institution that has not been able to make a case for investment in morale-building.

As with other precious characteristics of a healthy culture, trust is the product of leader behavior and rational policies. It cannot be ordered. An assumption of mutual trust within an institution is priceless. Trust does remain, however, a somewhat fragile commodity.

Once Upon a Time, Long, Long Ago…

…I was having discussions with company commanders in my first few weeks as a division commander. It was enjoyable for me and, I hoped, useful for them. A tank company commander asked me about comparing records of gunnery scores from the famed Tank Gunnery Table 8 and other onerous means of attempting to assess crew proficiency. He said, "General, it is not really fair to compare one set of gunnery results with another. Changing weather and visibility and conditions of the ground can make one run more difficult than another just a few hours apart."

I made a not-uncommon mistake of replying both too quickly and inadequately. I think I was pleasant, perhaps smiling, but my response was too self-oriented. I said, "Well, you know, I have commanded three companies and a separate armor brigade, and been deputy commander of the Armor Center and an assistant division commander of an armored division. Why do you think I don't understand that different conditions can make statistical comparisons questionable?" My response was not so off-putting as to dampen continuing discussion, but almost. I could have just explained that I did understand and had always tried to keep statistical comparisons in perspective.

Obviously, the company commander was not sure he could trust my capacity to handle those statistics. Apparently, his doubt had developed from exposure over the years to a system that had handled such data in a rigid, unforgiving mode. We senior people, through policy and behavior, affect the institution's prevailing reputation for competence and trustworthiness.

More on trusting the institution next in Note 16.

Organizational decision-making can proceed no faster than
the prevailing speed of mutual trust. Frank C. Sullivan, 2017[29]

---

[29] Sullivan is chairman and chief executive officer of RPM International, Inc., a highly-regarded leader and student of leadership.

Trusting the Institution—or Not

Maintaining trust within and about an institution in an era of skepticism regarding hierarchical organizations is both a critical task and a formidable challenge. The solution requires the institution—as represented by its senior leaders—to act consistently and clearly in harmony with professed values, and to explain expeditiously any apparent deviation from those values.

If individuals inside or outside view the institution as incompetent, uncaring, or hypocritical, they will disconnect. The first response may be simple disappointment and mild alienation. If the uncertainty and discomfort persist—if individual members conclude that the institution is not living up to its part of the contract—they will look for and, maybe reluctantly, find a life elsewhere. In the military, leaving the institution means leaving the profession. There is only one Army; it's not like moving from Bank of America to Citi.

Disappointment regarding institutional value discord is only one of many reasons for leaving military service. At issue here is the need for the institution to solidify and perpetuate trust by adhering to espoused values. This, and only this, will enable it to attract and retain the high-quality volunteers needed to carry out its responsibilities.

Naturally, higher headquarters are always suspect. They are a convenient target for complaints of varying credibility. (I recall a friend's story after he spent a day riding with a mechanized infantry squad on maneuvers. A good bunch of soldiers, they did feel that "them folks up at platoon headquarters is just out of touch!") In any case, a substantial degree of informed mutual trust is necessary to harness and focus organizational energy.

Soldiers are expected to do their best, respond faithfully to orders, keep physically and mentally fit, develop their skills, and work as part of a team. The parent institution, in turn, has the obligation to provide the best possible training and armaments, promulgate coherent codes of behavior, discipline its members, create healthy command climates, craft a reliable system for promotion and assignment, provide relevant education, offer suitable income and health services, and assist families.

All leaders have a primary obligation to faithfully support the institution and its legitimate priorities. They behave and make decisions in a way that reinforces key values. Further, good leaders support the chain of command and the institution by never complaining to subordinates about orders or policies. They take the initiative to remedy the situation, make timely suggestions to the boss, take notes for future action, and self-check to make sure that they are not in fact part of the problem.

One example of the need for mutual trust and confidence is in composing and implementing battlefield rules of engagement (ROE). This critical, complex institutional product must be crafted and articulated to make sense at all echelons. The institution rightly expects subordinate leaders to faithfully comply. The leader in the field expects to receive guidelines that are rational and practicable. The reliable field implementation of sensitive policies depends considerably on individuals trusting the system.

Designing policies that presume honesty and good judgment in their execution is also an institutional obligation. Any implied distrust downward may be more corrosive than suspicion of "them folks up at platoon headquarters." Policies and procedures reeking of distrust keep sneaking into the system. They are often the residue of hasty response to some mishap that "must never happen again." They often lay within legitimate policy initiatives, have only a faint aroma of distrust, and live beneath the radar of efforts to detect dysfunction.

Examples of institutional distrust of its membership include everything from a first sergeant having to leave a military ID card with the attendant to check out a basketball to the colonel graduating from the War College who must have somebody initial departure papers confirming there are no unreturned library books. Now the other side of this is that when the basketball or the library book is missing, there must be consequences. But bureaucracy unchained in its search for efficiency can overwhelm the elegance of a profession.

Bright, dedicated people in the twenty-first century need—and deserve—the assurance that their senior leaders abide by the rules of the game and support, by personal example and policy directive, the values of the institution. Most of them do. Here is a reminder or pledge for senior military leaders. I will to the best of my ability:

- offer candid professional advice to military and civilian leaders
- provide clear purpose, mission, and priorities to organizations
- generate resources adequate for assigned missions
- provide the best training, equipment, and weaponry to our soldiers
- maintain organizational climates that are supportive, ethical, and rational
- ensure that policies and pronouncements assume subordinate professionalism
- announce decisions in time for units and individuals to act effectively
- promote individuals based on both character and competence
- protect subordinate units from unwarranted intrusion
- craft rules of engagement, mindful of strategic goals, that support tactical mission accomplishment and honor our pledge to leave no soldier behind
- hold leaders accountable for policies, behavior, and outcomes
- keep in touch with reality on the ground
- hold all soldiers to high professional standards and take any appropriate disciplinary action regardless of grade, position, gender, or ethnicity

Once Upon a Time, Long, Long Ago …

… we were receiving routinely remarkable support from the US Air Force. Courage and competence were all over the place. Our missions were clear. At that same time, elements in the Pentagon far away seemed confused in their hierarchy of priorities.

One day, our savvy major general boss asked how things were going. Incoming fire and casualties were decreasing. I said, "Things are looking pretty good. But I could use a cold beer."

"Roger, out," he said. He was not much for talk. Also, he knew that using the secure channel on the radio ate up our battery. The Air Force was dropping about a hundred tons of ammo and supplies per day at that time, with maybe 85 or 90 percent falling inside our perimeter.

About ten days later, parachuting in with the beans and bullets were a few hundred pounds of ice and several dozen cases of beer! Most of the beer disappeared quickly on the drop zone, and most of the ice didn't survive the drop and the ninety-degree temperatures. I shared a warm can of beer the next day.

About two weeks later a supporting night-bombing run went wrong—an accident that unfortunately happens now and then. Somehow misguided from a ground beacon, aircraft flew across the middle of our area and dropped about eight 500-pound bombs. Way off target, they obliterated two battalion command posts. I said knock off beacon-assisted air strikes.

About two weeks later from the Pentagon came a cluster of officers from some inspector general's office. They did their inspecting from some in-country headquarters, our battle area not being conveniently accessible. Also, I found out that there was no need for them to collect data from us about the mishap. They were not checking how to prevent future night-bombing errors. They were collecting evidence for possible disciplinary proceedings against our warrior boss who ordered the "unauthorized" ice and beer drop!

Institutions sometimes need to lighten up. They also need to review the priorities of their priorities. Or, as stated in the company commander's philosophy in Note 8, "There is a difference between 'cutting slack' and 'looking the other way.'"

I cannot expect loyalty from the Army if I do not give it. General George C. Marshall

Note

17

The Toxic Leader Phenomenon

The toxic leader phenomenon, a debilitating artifact of all hierarchical institutions, is receiving renewed attention. "Toxic" is but one form of "destructive" leadership; the other categories are discussed in Chart 3 to follow. Recent attention to the longstanding issue is probably the result of recognition that in an era demanding highly efficient and effective organizations every bit of human energy is needed.

Human potential cannot be optimized unless there is a rational organizational climate—and toxic leaders mess that up. Due in part to successful efforts over the past forty years in explaining what good leadership looks like, troops today have high expectations.

The first priority in the toxic leader discussion is to define the term and distinguish *toxic* from *tough*. Toxic is characterized by dysfunctional behavior. It can be measured by collective subordinate assessments reflecting the impact on morale. Toxic leaders are abusive, unreasonable, capricious, and distrusting. Their most conspicuous dysfunctional impact is disruption of the flow of information: they do not listen, and they typically shoot the carrier of bad news. Innovation is sabotaged. The ultimate outcome of toxic leadership—if indeed it is "leadership" at all—is reduced capability to accomplish the two fundamental missions: win in battle and sustain a healthy force.

The hard-driving, results-oriented, sometimes insensitive gruff commander who is focused on unit before self, is hard but fair, and shares hardship and glory is not toxic.

Good leaders come in a variety of shapes and personalities. The troops know that. They do not ask for perfection.

Toxic leaders exist in every hierarchical bureaucracy because criteria for promotion typically focus on measurable short-term results that the toxic personality often produces. Frequently those results are gained by inappropriate behaviors that discourage subordinates, stifle innovation, and create stress. Most individuals identified as toxic leaders are intelligent and energetic. They are interpersonally skilled when relating to the boss. Some are aware of the negative impact of their behavior and are unconcerned. Some are in denial about the impact of their style.

Because the true toxic leader may be a prisoner of hard-wired drives, it is unlikely that such a personality will respond to education or training. The long-term institutional solution must be to identify and reject those individuals as soon as there are data pointing to a high probability of toxicity. This is an uncomfortable reality for an institution committed to the idea that leaders are made, not born, and eager to give individuals the benefit of the doubt. But that generously humane sometimes politically correct approach often disregards reality.

When things go wrong, competent leaders start looking at themselves first as a possible source of the problem. The toxic leader's response is different. Perhaps the entire unit would be assembled and berated for their obvious failure. While assembling the troops to hear good news from the boss can lift spirits, assembling them to be castigated is never productive. If in fact the whole operation is in internal disarray, the boss must be the prime suspect.

A More Definitive Look: Taxonomy of Destructive Leaders

We have a generally accepted vocabulary when describing good leaders. It would be helpful to think in more definitive terms about bad or destructive leaders. First, we might agree that destructive leaders are those whose presence leads to significantly decreased organizational effectiveness. The "destructives" could then be divided into five subgroups, plus an additional group covering spectacular misbehavior.

These types evolve in complex ways not fully understood. There must be significant influence from inherent drives, possibly compounded by poor parenting, painful job experience, and examples set by poor prior leaders. The destructive cadre may represent from 10 to nearly 20 percent of senior leaders as viewed from the subordinate perspective. This is a reflection of the fact that our current systems for selecting leaders in both the private and public sectors are relatively primitive, even as they are receiving increased analysis and scrutiny.

While the 10 to nearly 20 percent figure, compiled from a variety of surveys varies widely among and within organizations, those average percentages have persisted for decades. Meanwhile, there are organizations of significant size with no indication of toxic leader presence. Toxic presence is not automatic but still all too common.

Since selection systems in most institutions rely exclusively on input from results-oriented bosses, leaders who destroy the heart of the organization while achieving spectacular immediate results can get regularly promoted.

While all toxic leaders are destructive to the organization, not all destructive leaders are toxic. A description of different kinds of inept leadership would be helpful to discussion and analysis. Chart 3 ahead offers one possibility.

> I have seen some extremely good colonels become very
> bad generals. Maurice de Saxe,[30] 1732

---

[30] Maurice de Saxe, 1696–1750, became marshal general of France after heroic service starting with his enlistment as a soldier at age twelve.

Chart 3. Categorization of destructive leaders

Subgroup	Destructive description	Subgroup %*	Remediation
I Incompetent manager	Cannot move from tactical to strategic; inadequate cognitive or emotional fitness prevents timely, sound decisions; does not build teams; cannot formulate or promulgate a coherent vision.	**10%?**	Some change may be possible from enhanced self-awareness, managerial and leadership education, and coaching—if the requisite intellect is there.
II Affable non-participant	Interpersonally skilled but lacks the assertiveness and energy required to lead; provides little or no guidance; avoids decisions; fond of meetings and discussion; attentive to visitors.	**20%?**	Some change may be possible from enhanced self-awareness along with sustained coaching, but only if he has a strong interest in becoming a leader.
III Insensitive driven achiever	Bright and energetic; consumed by need for accomplishment; creates a frenetic climate and micromanages; oblivious to the needs of others; rarely intentionally abusive.	**35%?**	Change would be difficult, but not impossible. Enhanced self-awareness plus coaching along with strong organizational incentives for change could do it. May be the most amenable subgroup for change.

IV **Toxic self-centered abuser**	Usually bright, energetic, goal-oriented, boss-focused; often gets spectacular results; arrogant, abusive, intemperate, irascible, poor listener; a distrusting micromanager.	**30%?**	The narcissist seems unlikely to significantly modify behavior. The practical question is how much organizational pain is worth any unique contributions he brings to justify his retention.
V **Criminal**	Usually bright, energetic, sometimes charismatic; cheats, steals, entices, misrepresents, defrauds.	**5%?**	Change would be for all practical purposes impossible in the near term—and in effect irrelevant.
X **Scandalous misbehaver**	Variety of intellects and energy levels; often hard-working and seen as a "good leader"; poor judgment and lack of self-control lead to conspicuous incidents, such as substance abuse, unacceptable sexual behavior, improper relationships with subordinates.	Not related to leader style.	Disreputable acts by a senior leader typically result in rejection by the organization, with limited capacity for repair. Although some cases of substance abuse may be treatable, it is difficult for a senior leader to regain credibility and influence after a spectacular misbehavior.

*Note: These percentage estimates are within the small group of destructive leaders, not within the overall group of organizational leaders.

Neither the toxic leader nor the leader whose behavior is simply unprofessional—the one who drinks too much, hits on subordinates, has his aide buy bracelets for his girlfriend, expects motorcycle escorts when going to the post office, or allows his wife to terrorize shop employees—escapes the awareness and judgment of his direct staff. Outrageous behavior by a senior leader never comes as a surprise to the troops. Only the boss is caught unaware.

This is but another justification for periodically—perhaps annually—gathering input from the immediate staff on senior officer behavior. (The "More definitive climate survey" in Appendix A would do the trick.) For the vast majority of senior officers, the results will be good news and a useful exercise for both the subordinates and the boss. For that small but conspicuous group who made it to senior levels in spite of unprofessional behavior, it could be a major basis for actions that terminate their careers.

One question lurks in the background of this discussion: "Is the toxic individual in question so crucial to our productivity that we must put up with such behavior?" More often than not, there is a substitute leader who can both supervise building the next super-laser and also maintain a healthy work environment. If not, and the mission-essential genius is truly unique and indispensable, the boss has the obligation to provide a barrier to minimize abuse of subordinates, alienation of peers, and erosion of teamwork.

Ongoing initiatives give considerable hope that the institution is gaining on the problem. Earlier behavioral feedback for development, a more sophisticated array of information provided to selection boards, and hopefully data from various assessment tools and evaluative exercises can guarantee improvement if not ensure 100 percent success. Then the toxic leader issue might fade into stories about the "old days when we had some real SOBs to deal with."

The only credible response to the problem rests in the screening and selection processes. Early identification of potentially toxic personalities is increasingly possible. This requires collecting organized perceptions from those who best gauge leader style: the subordinates. At the very early stage of admission into the profession, in recruit or officer training, peer observations also can provide a unique perspective. (See George Reed's *Tarnished*[31] for a more extensive coverage of toxic leadership.)

> It is exceptional and difficult to find in one man all the qualities necessary for a great general. What is most desirable, and which instantly sets a man apart, is that his intelligence or talent are balanced by his character or courage. Napoleon, 1831

---

[31] Reed, *Tarnished*. There are powerful insights here about more than toxic leadership. This is a thoughtful review of important aspects of the culture by one of the primary thought-leaders in the field.

Note

18

Born versus Made and Cognitive Ability

Individuals are born with certain predispositions and aptitudes. These inherent characteristics can be molded, reinforced, or diminished to some degree by experience and education. How to enhance inherent strength and remedy natural weakness remains a challenge for institutions and professions. Officer education and training programs may be the most effective large-scale leader-development operations in America.

Discomfort with the Reality of Inherent Differences

While some of us can never make the Olympics, compose a symphony, or become a Rhodes scholar, the normal range of human aptitudes offers a variety of leadership opportunities. Even the few born with all the right stuff need effort by self and others to take advantage of those gifts. That "right stuff" for a military leader includes intellectual, emotional, and physical capabilities.

Americans cheer for *made* over *born*. We cherish a level playing field. We like to believe all candidates can make the team if they try hard. The unreality of that premise is pretty much accepted in the sports and music worlds. The idea of directly screening or categorizing based on cognitive ability is viewed by some as unfair.

At some point, it is. Cognitive capacity and emotional resilience are considerably more nature than nurture. We indirectly screen for intellectual competence by comparing levels of productivity and academic success, as incomplete as those measures sometimes are. We screen similarly by requiring pre-commissioning academic certification.

Military schools often award grades for academic instruction, although their grading methodology or standards may have a weakness: very few ever fail. We flunk candidates from Airborne, Sniper, Sapper, Ranger, or Aviation school, but seem hesitant to enforce academic standards for commissioned officers.

Formal education may have played only a minor role in developing the constitution, confidence, or insight of world-class leaders. VMI did not create George Marshall, nor did West Point create Grant, Lee, MacArthur, Patton, Ridgway, or Eisenhower. No doubt these institutions—like many others in America--nourished an aptitude for and confirmed an interest in leadership while honing decision-making skills. The examples of these giants along with the likes of Alexander, Wellington, Napoleon, Nelson, and Washington are not justification for abandoning leader development. But they are monuments to the reality that inborn characteristics make a difference. Searching for and enhancing those characteristics is increasingly necessary to sustain twenty-first century institutional excellence.

Brainpower and Leader Competence

Competent, timely decision-making, particularly under conditions in our world of advertised complexity and ambiguity, is driven in great part by cognitive ability—the capacity to think quickly and logically, to put disparate pieces together and see the big picture, to put information to work. The required level of cognitive capacity obviously varies by position. While a platoon leader's duties may call for emotional and physical resources similar to those of the brigade or division commander, the intellectual requirements at higher levels are significantly different.[32] While all effective leaders at higher levels must be quick thinkers, all quick thinkers are not effective leaders.[33]

---

[32] Stamp, "Longitudinal Research into Methods of Assessing Managerial Potential." This scholarly piece is useful for those who want to dive more deeply into an approach describing and assessing competencies required at different organizational levels.

[33] Ulmer, "Military Leadership into the 21st Century." This article provides further coverage of the role of intellect and the various types of knowledge, competence, and learning from the perspective of an organizational leader.

Fortunately, the relationship between thinking skills and doing skills seems comfortable. We have produced numerous strategic thinkers who earned high decorations in battle, including the Distinguished Service Cross and Medal of Honor. Excellent performers in combat typically have higher than average intellect.

A study just after the Korean War identified characteristics that discriminated between individuals who were rated in combat (by their peers and immediate commanders) as either extremely effective or extremely ineffective. The most pronounced and differentiating characteristics were first intelligence and second emotional stability. While this study, titled "Fighter I," was done decades ago, there is no indication that human nature has changed in the interim.[34] A kind of meta-analysis in 1980, "Soldier Capability—Army Combat Effectiveness Study (SCACE)" came to the conclusion that measurable intellect and level of education both made a profound difference in soldier effectiveness.[35]

> The nation that insists on drawing a line between the fighting man and the thinking man is liable to find its fighting done by fools and its thinking by cowards. Sir William Butler, 1838-1910

---

[34] Egbert et. al., "Fighter I: A Study of Effective and Ineffective Combat Performance." In the summer of 1953, shortly after leaving the battlefield, 647 infantrymen were interviewed and 345 were chosen to complete the surveys and interviews. The study's findings mirrored those of a related study by Mitchell M. Berkum et. al., conducted in a simulated combat environment, that found "general intelligence, reading comprehension, and mechanical aptitude" as the top differentiating characteristics. At high or low levels, appropriate intelligence counts.

[35] Toomepuu, "SCACE Study." This excellent 1980 overview incorporated findings from several prior efforts and concluded both technical and "fighter" capability strongly correlate with measurable intelligence.

In the 2004 and 2010 studies of critical leader behaviors of division commanders discussed in Note 12, two behaviors of highly regarded leaders that kept appearing were *making sound decisions* and *keeping cool.*

Assessing and Enhancing Intellectual Skills

A variety of challenging courses, such as Ranger or Special Forces, identify and access capacity for tactical leadership through evaluation in a variety of situations. We rely on the collective evaluation of performance—by instructors, lane-graders, and observer-controllers—to measure immediate accomplishment, with all its implications for future potential. These efforts are augmented by periodic performance reports. While successful completion of such rigorous programs requires both thinking and doing skills, and while rating officers capture perceptions of intellectual competence in performance reports, our Army has no direct, reliable measurement of pre-or post-commissioning cognitive ability. If tests were devised to measure intellectual acuity, the state of the art has advanced to the point where their results should not confuse dyslexic impairments with intellectual limitations as happened during General George Patton's West Point years. Our limited knowledge of mental ability in the force is quite unlike our data base on physical readiness, and not comparable to the attention devoted to updating physical fitness testing and data collection—which is still not an institutional strength. While the process of assessing cognitive ability in its various forms and translating that into useful data remains a challenge, it is within the range of the possible. Such a program could assist in efforts to recruit and retain intellectually gifted officers.[36] A delicate but urgent topic.

The argument that the composite of intellectual hurdles for college graduation and completion of basic or even advanced service schools confirms adequate intellect for

---

[36] Gerras and Wong, "America's Army: Measuring Quality Soldiers." These authors have provided several insightful and provocative studies covering critical personnel and leadership issues. Their writings on ethics, climates, and the impact of continuous deployments on morale and retention deserve a hard look.

career progression seems shaky. Graduation academic class rankings, valued in particular because they represent a composite of intellect and perseverance, are surely helpful. If we did have a pre-commissioning final academic examination—a sort of bar exam-- for four-year ROTC scholarship recipients and West Point graduates, the leaders of Cadet Command or the U.S. Military Academy would have a lot of explaining to do were there any failures.

There has been a taint of anti-intellectualism with the culture of most military institutions. That genesis might be vague but the impact cannot have been helpful. Lloyd George, who served as British Prime Minister from 1916-1822, noted that "The military mind…regards thinking as a form of mutiny!" In the shadow of the tragic blunders of WWI, that might not be surprising. Recent thinkers, COL Lloyd Matthews in particular, noted that remnants of belittling the contemplative officer still exist.[37] If that is even partially true, we risk going to battle without the best firepower our nation has to offer.

Leader Responsibility for Enhancing and Retaining Brainpower

The institutional solution for producing effective leaders is to attract talent and then manage that pool through assessment and motivation to meet organizational needs. Policies addressing those institutional challenges and their solutions are not open to much modification by junior leaders. However, leaders at all levels have irreplaceable, heavy responsibilities for reinforcing institutional systems of socialization, education, and selection.

Senior leaders are responsible for:

- creating climates that motivate competent officers to remain in service

---

[37] Matthews, "The Uniformed Intellectual and His Place in the American Army." COL Matthews was our leading scholar on the subject and his writing is essential background for any discussion of this cultural issue.

- supporting personnel policies that lead to prompt elimination of unqualified officers by any measure—intelligence, integrity, behavior—so that competent professionals are not disappointed by unwillingness of the institution to enforce standards
- supporting individual writing projects apart from formal schooling
- being candid in reporting intellectual strengths and weaknesses of subordinates
- maintaining high standards for intellectual work
- coaching subordinates and supporting their efforts for continuing education
- making an effort to retain and properly assign the bright, dedicated officers who are uncomfortable commanding troops but superb planners or technicians
- setting the example for excellence in all aspects of leadership

Junior leaders are responsible for:

- coaching subordinates and supporting their efforts for continuing education
- setting the example for excellence in all aspect of leadership
- noting the need to build mental as well as physical muscle, and that our profession expects intellectual competence as well as physical and moral courage
- taking great care in evaluating subordinate proficiency and aptitude
- explaining the long-term advantages of being a professional soldier.

To dominate on the battlefield of the future… the Army must invest in its people.[38] *The Human Dimensions White Paper*, 2014.

---

[38] "Human Dimensions White Paper," 2014, 7.

Thoughts on General Officer (and CEO) Leadership

How generals lead today compared to yesterday, how generals compare with their corporate counterparts, and whether or not the right people are promoted to those grades are more than interesting questions. The "right people" question is the most important. An institution's selection and promotion methodology determine its vitality, productivity, and reputation.

Books have been written about generalship for a long time. Many are worth reading. Personality and performance data on generals and their civilian counterparts have been collected at research and educational organizations like the Center for Creative Leadership (CCL.) Military educational activities such as the Army War College or the Army's Center for Army Leadership or the National Defense University have collected information that can inform policies for selecting and educating general officers.

In one example of sustained data collection, Dr. David Campbell and other CCL scholars concluded that Army generals compare favorably as leaders with executives in the corporate world as seen from views of their subordinates.[39] Generals also compare favorably in the area of cognitive ability, although measures used for that comparison were not definitive at the upper end of the mental ability spectrum.

While senior officers display considerable variations in style, common characteristics emerge. A high percentage of generals—and CEOs—have personality profiles that tend toward dependable, confident, goal-oriented, predictable, competitive, responsible, externally-driven performance, with all the potential strengths and limitations those characteristics imply. Physical courage appears commonplace. Typical hard-charging and dominating tendencies may have been moderated somewhat by increased intuition and empathy among those selected for three- and four-star rank.[40] The institution has particular responsibilities for attending to their physical and emotional health, understanding that goal-oriented behaviors common among strong leaders can lead to physical or emotional exhaustion.[41]

In evaluating leader effectiveness, subordinates bring a unique, essential perspective. While not typically capable of assessing the strategic planning or financial expertise

---

[39] Campbell, "The Psychological Profiles of Brigadier Generals." The original data were compiled in 1987 and updated in 1996 at CCL with no significant changes in personality profiles. Informal observations from faculties at CCL and the Army War College do not indicate a meaningful difference in these characteristics in recent years, but a current review would be warranted. In an August 30, 1987, presentation before Division 14, American Psychological Association, in New York, Dr. Campbell noted that "general officers we have now are ... bright, well-educated, experienced, responsible, and well indoctrinated into democratic ways ... In that regard, we are a fortunate society." He described their typical personality as "dominant, competitive, action-oriented ... drawn naturally to physically adventuresome military activities ... with high needs for control ... and achievement through conformity." These characteristics might be qualified a bit by the data assembled by Dr. T. O. Jacobs indicating that at the three- and four-star level, there may be more inner-directed and intuitive tendencies in the personalities.

[40] Jacobs, *A Guide to the Strategic Leader Development Inventory*. Dr. Jacobs writes from the combined and somewhat unique perspective of a recognized scholar and a perceptive observer/consultant to Army personnel systems.

[41] Kane, "Total Volunteer Force (Summary Report)." A bold, comprehensive study. The book, Total Volunteer Force, Lessons from the US Military on Leadership Culture and Talent Management, was published in June, 2017.

of the boss, they are experts at evaluating basic leadership. We have over the decades produced many leaders of the "I would want my sons and daughters to go to war with" category. Our institution has also produced some of the previously noted toxic variety who make life miserable for everyone but themselves. A former Army psychologist, Lieutenant Colonel Larry Ingraham, PhD, noted, "A personnel system that cannot differentiate between the revered and the despised has some kind of problem!"[42]

Why discuss generals at all? Because all the Army's future generals are currently lieutenants or captains or majors. They might take notes so that "if I become one, I will be sure to do this and never do that!" We examine closely our promotion procedures because generals once selected are not always easy to teach, control, or retrain. Every war shows the challenge of keeping division commanders on a common sheet of administrative and strategic music.

We at all levels have a key role in maintaining a reliable promotion system that ultimately determines who becomes a senior leader: complete every fitness report with all possible objectivity, including noting the uncomfortable truths of limited future potential; do our best to exemplify and explain what good leadership looks like; create a climate that encourages promising future senior leaders to remain in the profession; and be intolerant of ethical misbehavior by anybody, including high-profile personalities. The following could be useful when dealing with generals, or when you become one:

- Generals are busy, get briefed too much, and have a lot of folks wanting face time.
- They have multiple bosses—even if only one is officially designated.
- Most have had limited conversations with subordinates. Our culture discourages informal exchanges. Subordinates can brief and respond, but they don't usually converse. As a result, generals too often are ignorant of "what everybody knows."
- Most have fond memories of "how it used to be when I was a …" that are both precious and hazardous. They need their relevant past experience updated.

> There are three pillars of general officer leadership: courage, creative intelligence, and physical fitness. J. F. C. Fuller

---

[42] From comments by Lieutenant Colonel Ingraham to author and others present, circa 1970.

- It is rare that they know their subordinates as well as they think they do.
- They can be greatly assisted, or misinformed and shielded from bad news, by their immediate staff.
- They may believe themselves approachable while in reality are intimidating.

Better generals share the following characteristics:

- They know how to really listen (and in so doing, get others to talk openly).
- They don't make more decisions than they need to. They control the impulse to always jump in and take charge, especially when qualified subordinates are present.
- They have a sense of humor (a word or smile can change everybody's day).
- They first check their own policies and behaviors when hunting for the source of a disaster (another reason to have an immediate staff that dares to be candid).
- They come down hard and fast on anybody—including comrades from past battles—who behaves unethically.
- They rarely keep people waiting in the outer office (the best opportunity to check both personal thoughtfulness and the quality of the gatekeepers.)
- They never glance down to their personal pad/phone when being briefed.
- They know and appreciate the difference between disagreement and disloyalty (not easy for strong personality types.)
- They know when to give a pat on the back and when not to (authentic thanks remains a powerful motivator; undeserved pats spoil the moment.)
- They resist the lure of tactics when they should be focusing on strategy. (How about a note clearly visible each day: "I promise to finish my work before doing somebody else's!")
- They know how to use, inspire, and support a staff, providing them the same courtesy and attention given commanders and personal staff.

- They speak for themselves and don't use a third party to give bad news. (Bad news should be given in person, not over the net or via the deputy or chief of staff.)
- They don't let their personal staff protect them from reality. (Long-tenure or repeat personal staffers are particularly suspect.)
- They recognize that upon promotion to general, scrutiny of their behavior becomes intense; impact of their behavior increases dramatically; and reliable feedback about their behavior decreases significantly.

In order to best execute their enormous range of responsibilities, general officers (or CEOs) improve life for themselves and others by tuning up their leader behavior. Our military services in recent years have drawn up extensive plans for their continuing education and orientation. Only decades ago, such post-graduate intervention might have been dismissed as unnecessary or even disparaging.

Many leadership malfunctions at mid and senior levels are driven by ignorance of the impact of one's behavior on others. This along with a weak assessment of—or disinterest in—their own strengths and weaknesses is a potent mix. Unchained ambition and toxicity sometimes enter also into the failure equation.

Truly bizarre behavior at senior levels may in fact be in statistical decline, but spectacular incidents draw a crowd along with special public and institutional concern when military values appear to have been abandoned. There is a bright side to such public concern and disappointment: it confirms that expectations for military officer professionalism remain high.

As mentioned, few senior leaders, military or civilian, fail for lack of strategic vision or technical skills. From Army studies of the 1970s,[43] Center for Creative Leadership research in the 1980s,[44] and macro summaries of causes of executive derailment, the data are clear: flaws in interpersonal skills, empathy, and trustworthiness remain the major contributing factors.[45]

---

[43] USAWC, *Study on Military Professionalism;* and USAWC, *Leadership for the 1970s.* The July 1971 *Leadership for the 1970s* was an offshoot of the *Study on Military Professionalism* directed by Chief of Staff General Westmoreland and published on June 30, 1970. It was designed to explore the reasons for defects in the Army's professional climate as revealed in the professionalism study. It includes what may have been one of the first studies to capture perspective from self, subordinate, and superior, a "trifocal" perspective. It portrays the difference between what I think I am doing and what observers see me doing, what we identified as "perception shortfall," along with measures of "performance shortfall" (the difference between what I am doing and what I should be doing). Each of these measures was provided for six different grade groups, from junior NCO to senior field grade officers. (We had additional data for general officers, but that didn't make the cut for either quantitative sampling technique reliability or reluctance to talk about generals—probably some of both.) Of all the Army leadership studies to which I have contributed between 1970 and 2015, this one is the best for providing practical advice for leaders at all levels. Why it has never been replicated is beyond me.

[44] McCall, *The Lessons of Experience.* This noted 1988 work produced at CCL remains relevant. The components of executive failure have not changed. Interpersonal skills and problems with integrity far outweigh technical incompetence as the key ingredient leading to "derailment."

[45] Noer, *Keeping Your Career on Track.* This 2016 book by an experienced scholar and practitioner is packed with insight relevant in all organizations. It is not possible to read it without doing some personal reflection.

For new generals: A possible pledge when pinning on the stars

Now a general officer, I acknowledge gratefully this singular opportunity for future service, and recognize therein my profound obligation as a steward of the military profession and its code of professional ethics.

By practicing physical and moral courage, in battle and elsewhere, I will endeavor to inspire those qualities in others. I will continue to improve my knowledge and practice of the profession of arms, being a patient listener as well as a decisive leader of character. Indebted to the American People who trust us with the lives of their sons and daughters, I will lead with impartiality and justice, ensuring that every individual under my authority is treated with respect and fairness, and properly trained and prepared for the assigned duty.

Recognizing that candor is the life-blood of a credible institution, I will speak the unvarnished truth to superiors, subordinates, and the American people. I will command, coach, and supervise without invading the legitimate prerogatives of trusted military and civilian subordinates, explaining the intent of my orders with unmistakable clarity while encouraging subordinate initiative in their execution. I will strive to be a thoughtful and prudent steward of the precious national resources placed under my care. I will hold myself and my subordinates accountable for both methods and results.

Aware that in the public eye I represent members of all our Armed Forces, I will be mindful of possible implications of all my actions. I will continue to put loyalty to the highest moral principles and the United States of America above loyalty to individuals, organizations, and my personal interest.

Notes from the Notes of Part 3

PART 4

Reinforcing and Respecting the Chain of Command

One of the most serious phases now confronting ... our service is the constant interference with [the troop commander] by ... post commanders who take upon themselves to prescribe minutely the ... method of instruction of his command.

The Cavalry Journal, March 1911

Centralization, Empowerment, and Responsibility

Centralization of authority comes naturally to bureaucracy. Real or imagined policies preventing subordinate initiative remain a major source of frustration. Finding the proper balance between essential centralization and desirable empowerment of subordinates remains a challenge. When operational success depends heavily on subordinate initiative, as with most contemporary operations, finding such balance becomes a necessity. Inappropriate centralization of authority penalizes doubly. It reduces the ability of subordinate leaders to exploit their skill and situational awareness, and it diverts focus and energy at higher echelons from their unique responsibilities.

Clarifying who has the authority to make what kind of decision is worth discussion in any organization and at every level, from platoon to army, and in every staff. The time to do it is well before action begins. Erroneous assumptions about the boundaries of action--the limitations on authority—are common even in good organizations. The issue is sensitive, emotional, central to a coherent climate, and too often not open for discussion

Institutional Recognition of a Continuing Problem

Granting subordinates the authority to accomplish assigned missions has long been recognized as necessary for a high-performing organization. However, attempted solutions to align authority with responsibility have taken hold only sporadically. Remembering that the default position of all bureaucracies is "stupid," leaders have to push to achieve proper balance.

Crafting and monitoring policies to provide necessary authority at subordinate levels is not remarkably sophisticated in principle. But it becomes complicated in practice. Upward creep of authority can be fueled by a simple lack of senior leader awareness of how complex organizations should work—how processes, policies, assumptions, and communications systems combine to influence outcomes. Well-intended policies can have a dysfunctional second or third-order impact. This aspect of organizational dynamics seems an obvious choice for expanded inclusion in the curriculum for officer education.

Decentralization is counterintuitive for some leaders. Abandoning the take-charge style that led to previous success can be disconcerting. Some reluctance to let go of the reins may be fostered by hypersensitivity to possible career-limiting mistakes on the part of subordinates. Some leaders just lack the energy or confidence or appetite to attack the status quo.

As mentioned, recent efforts in the U.S. Army to align authority with responsibility have been advertised under the Mission Command rubric. Articulating that approach absent supportive policies has not typically been successful. Too often, the doctrine has said "Decentralize, empower, and hold accountable," while policies de facto say "I'm not sure we trust you" or "Don't make any mistakes." When institutional doctrinal pronouncements are confronted with contrary local policies steeped in caution or doubt, local always wins.

Inappropriate centralization of tactical or training activities represents only a part of this cultural issue. In fact, decentralization in the administrative arena holds as much potential for strengthening organizational productivity as initiatives in field operations. When particular activities must be reported to higher headquarters without delay— for example, the percentage of assigned personnel who attend particular seminars— those absolutes move to the head of the list of non-reportable operational priorities whether deserved or not. Having an administrative Mission Command environment where end-states are described but methods are left to local commanders should be as important as the tactical Mission Command model. For example, in an administrative Mission Command mode, problems with sexual harassment or bullying might be dealt with by the following:

- explaining clearly the desired outcome
- providing resources to commanders sufficient to create the appropriate awareness, attitude, and disciplined response through whatever training and educational methods are chosen
- after an acceptable interval, acknowledging those commanders who meet standards and disciplining or relieving those who do not
- advertising the lessons learned

A relevant question is exactly what in the contemporary culture makes this basic managerial approach so difficult. Again, risk-averse routines in garrison can implant a mind-set that makes transfer to a Mission Command mode in the field uncomfortable if not impossible.[46]

Criteria for Decentralization

Decentralization is not designed to appease subordinates. It is a necessity in building an organization that exploits available brainpower, commitment, energy, creativity, and opportunity. What should be considered in correctly redistributing authority?

> Commanders delegate sufficient authority to Soldiers in the chain of command to accomplish their assigned duties, and commanders may hold these Soldiers responsible for their actions. AR 600-20, November 6, 2014

---

[46] Bass, *Platoon Readiness as a Function of Leadership, Platoon, and Company Cultures.* This 2000 study, in which I participated, indicated that habits and leader effectiveness measured in garrison generally predict platoon success in simulated combat.

The first question to ask is "are there lower headquarters that could perform the function satisfactorily?" A major factor here is the degree to which the senior commander—or those representing him—believe that only at the higher headquarters is there the combination of competence and commitment to carry out the task. Such common assumptions of unique capabilities are rarely contested. The principle of "Employ your command in accordance with its capabilities" is relevant here. Understanding the capacity of subordinate agencies and staffs to handle matters is as necessary as understanding the combat power and readiness of subordinate organizations. A few examples of typical opportunities to increase efficiency follow.

At a large installation, truck drivers had to be tested or retested for their licenses every two years. The test was relatively simple and did not require evaluator expertise unavailable in major subordinate organizations. But to ensure "uniformity" and "high standards," the traditional procedure required all drivers to be tested at one central—and inconveniently located—test station. This installation was home to hundreds of trucks, and lines at the central testing station were long and slow-moving.

The policy itself indicated a lack of trust in the competence or commitment of subordinate commanders. (It is worthwhile to decide which one is the driving factor.) When the policy was changed to permit major subordinate commanders to issue licenses, accidents did not increase, time was saved, and trust was enhanced. (If accidents due to driver error had increased, the commander responsible for driver testing should have been held accountable. Decentralization does not mean disengagement.)

Not too long ago, there was an imposed cut in manpower at various bases across the United States. The cuts were to come from installation management positions involving cutting the grass, securing the post, auditing accounts, keeping the library open, investigating accidents, staffing firing ranges, operating clubs, etc. The Washington headquarters specified the exact positions to be cut at every installation across the fruited plain. But circumstances among them differed greatly. Some needed a higher percentage of employees in certain categories than others, grass growing at different rates, etc. Local knowledge would have permitted intelligent allocation of the cuts while still eliminating the required number of spaces.

This violation of common sense must have emerged from a lack of information about the particulars of various installations, reinforced by an assumption that higher headquarters knew best. Apparently at higher headquarters, there was no confidence that left to their own discretion, subordinate elements would loyally and efficiently carry out the intended purpose.

A senior officer in the Pentagon thought colonels personally known to him had not been given assignments that best suiting their leadership potential. (Their potential turned out to be not quite what the general estimated, but that is another story.) That senior officer's solution was to move assignment authority from a subordinate personnel office, obviously not up to the task of caring for high-potential colonels, into the Pentagon. There, at higher headquarters, there would be suitable competence, commitment, and strategic perspective.

When moving that office upward, it is probable that the actual assignment decisions in the Pentagon were made by individuals who had neither more expertise nor more relevant data than those in the subordinate personnel office. And there is no doubt that there was diminished energy focused on those other strategic and coordinating issues that the Pentagon alone can address. The assumption that all decisions at a senior headquarters are inherently of higher quality than at lower does not pass the common sense test.

> Never tell people how to do things. Tell them what to do and they will surprise you with their ingenuity. General George S. Patton

Selecting the right individuals for company-level command remains a challenge. It is sometimes done today with great care: local board appearances, review of reputation and prior performance by contact with former commanders, probably a call to the top human resources office, and very importantly the assessment of current bosses and perhaps peers. The fact is that in the case of officers with only a few years of service, thoughtful local assessments of potential are more often than not more accurate to evaluations from afar based on seniority and available performance data. The level at which personnel decisions should be made should be based significantly on who has access to the best relevant information. In the case of selecting company-level commanders from the available pool, the considered opinions of the local commanders who will have those captains as subordinates are often the most reliable.

Selection of battalion-level commanders may be the most strategic single personnel decision in our Army. The triage of potential candidates should be a sophisticated, lengthy operation. The climates they create have enormous influence on the career decisions of their captains and lieutenants. It is at the battalion level that all institutional and personal policies come together and must be integrated, translated, filtered, and prioritized.

Faced with this challenge, and provided a staff of limited experience and often high turnover, that lieutenant colonel carries an awesome load. Years ago, battalion commanders were selected locally. Decisions were proposed by local colonels, approved by local generals, and confirmed by the Pentagon. That was decentralization of a key function. It sometime worked. But too often cronyism intervened. Further, even the most fair-minded and well-intentioned general knew the qualifications of only a small subset of available candidates.

In the 1970s, that selection process was elevated appropriately to Washington, where all eligible candidates were in the pool.[47] The process was improved but remains

---

[47] That decision of General Westmoreland was initiated in part by recommendations of the USAWC professionalism study, which he directed and then supported in spite of its embarrassing conclusions.

imperfect because available personnel files are often inadequate to confirm relative rankings among candidates for both character and competence. (A possible solution to the command selection process is at Appendix B.)

Empowerment—an Element of Decentralization

Empowerment is mainly defined by the perception of those intended to be empowered. It is the act of aligning authority with responsibility. ("Decentralization" is the passing of organizational responsibilities downward.) If subordinates believe they have the necessary authority and they feel empowered, they are usually right. If they feel improperly constrained or powerless, they may or may not be right. The subordinate may have by pronouncement or regulation more authority than imagined. In any case, the best way—perhaps the only way—to determine subordinate perceptions about having requisite authority is to ask.

The degree to which a subordinate feels comfortable approaching the boss to raise issues varies considerably based on the prevailing relationship. It also varies on what we might call the hierarchical distance between the two. The greatest such distance in commissioned-officer structure in line units is between company and battalion commander levels. There are years of difference in age and experience.

In contrast, the battalion commander may have essentially the same background as the brigade commander. The age and experience gap between a major general division commander and colonel brigade commanders is wide, but brigade commanders have considerable experience and maturity as well. Efforts to empower or improve communication should consider these hierarchical differences.

While subordinates often complain about inadequate guidance on mission and priorities, they may complain simultaneously about micromanagement. Actually, there is no incompatibility here. They want a clear mission and commander's intent as well as latitude in how they accomplish the mission.

Innovations designed to empower are difficult to implement. Empowerment initiatives—transferring authority downward and sometimes contradicting long-standing protocols—are counterintuitive in hierarchies. Such initiatives have to be explained and clearly supported by the boss in policy as well as pronouncement before they have a chance of surviving. Furthermore, some subordinates are demonstrably uncomfortable having to make decisions traditionally made by others. It seems possible that risk-aversion is a communicable disease, particularly in the downward direction.[48]

Measuring the degree of latitude perceived by subordinates is rarely done. It is a suitable topic to be included in inspector general assessments. A good survey instrument can help explain the details while enhancing the flow of communication. (See the example items in Chart 4 in Note 21 and the full version in Appendix A.)

When Not to Decentralize or Empower

Some prerogatives and standards are not suitable for decentralization. That truth is often applied indiscriminately as an excuse to retain power by those who fear that empowering subordinates will somehow result in lack of responsiveness, uncoordinated activities, violations of standard procedure, and general chaos. But any coherent plan for empowerment does not include permission to amend professional principles, modify loyalties, or reinterpret the commander's intent. In my experiments with the process, empowered commanders never went outside the bounds of propriety, abused their expanded latitude, or disobeyed orders.

There are technical standards as well as values that should not yield to individual discretion and initiative. There should be no creativity or personalization when the mechanic torques the bolts on the rotor; no initiative on published speed limits in the motor pool; no innovation about how we stand at the position of attention; no local

---

[48] Drath, *Why Leaders Have Trouble Empowering.* This study mentions a variety of human and institutional realities that explain why passing authority downward is not an intuitive behavior.

modification of "no alcohol on the firebase." Adherence to standards does not discourage appropriate decentralization and empowerment within a healthy climate. In summary, we empower subordinates unless:

- The leader has unique access to critical operational information that cannot be shared. (This should be rare in a healthy environment, but when it does pertain, it is reason enough.)
- Subordinates are of doubtful skill, perspective, or commitment. (This is rare in our organizations. If commanding a mix of individuals of unknown quality, however, it is reasonable to be prudent.)
- Subordinates are unwilling or incapable of assuming decision-making responsibilities. (This is also rare and not difficult to detect if an experienced boss and staff have their ears to the ground. This condition may be modified by training and trust enhancement.)
- The leader has not yet developed relationships and channels of communication that make empowerment a comfortable mode of operation.
- Laws or regulations prohibit. (Certain legal responsibilities of command may not be delegated.)

The self-empowerment common sense rule

Leaders in every kind of organization have broken rules and defied orders to get the job done. Insightful senior leaders understand the need for placing what makes sense at the moment supersedes rules, regulations, and orders. But institutions have difficulty promulgating institutional policies that develop a culture tolerating or encouraging rule-breaking while preserving law and order. The essence of the solution is mutual trust amid an assumption that if the action is clearly within the commander's intent and consistent with professional ethics it is justified.

At an October, 2016 U.S. Army Symposium in Washington, Army Chief of Staff Mark Milley commented that "A subordinate needs to understand that they have the freedom and they are empowered to disobey a specific order, a specific task, in order to accomplish the purpose. It takes a bit of judgment." It does take judgment, and a trust in the judgment of the boss as well. Its implementation requires a hard and sophisticated push against cultural risk-aversion. The fact that the topic is on the discussion list is a start.

Is the Commander Always Responsible for Everything?

It has been a longstanding foundation of military culture that commanders are responsible for whatever the organization does or does not do. That proper assertion deserves clarification and refinement. This is another vital element of military professionalism not unfamiliar to executives elsewhere. There are, however, reasonable limits to commander responsibility. The parameters of those limits deserve discussion.

The primary question is "who should be held responsible for what types of individual misbehavior or what types of organizational failure?" We do not worry quite so much about who should be held accountable for sharing or celebrating organizational success! For some personality types, sharing success can be just as difficult as accepting blame.

It may be fair to say that a general feeling is that junior commanders are often held accountable for mistakes while senior commanders are let off the hook. While that could be more perception than reality it is not a trivial issue. How far up or down the chain of command should we go to hold one or more commanders responsible? Is a corps commander at fault for a brigade unprepared for maneuvers at a national training center? Is a battalion commander at fault for sexual harassment in one of the companies after being in command for two months? After being in command for six months? Is the company commander responsible if nobody in the company qualified for the Expert Infantryman badge? What level commanders are responsible for a fire team mistakenly engaging friendly forces?

There seem to be at least these components of this complex issue in determining if a commander, or commanders, should be held responsible:

- whether or not the commander took reasonable steps in policy, education, or training to prevent the disaster
- whether or not the commander should have known of the specific circumstances that caused the disaster and taken direct action to defuse the situation
- whether or not the commander had created a climate that contributed to the event
- whether or not the commander had the authority and opportunity to intervene

The disaster in question could range from a failure to commit his reserve and lose the battle or failure to stop firing on unarmed civilians or failure to have all the troops take anti-malarial medication or pass the aircraft readiness inspection or have 100 percent of the troops attend financial planning seminars or submit the budget on time or prevent motorcycle accidents or prevent fraud at the Hunting and Fishing Club or prevent cheating on rifle range scores. How the disaster is handled has a considerable impact on the trustworthiness of the institution.

This issue presents another opportunity for both the educational system and the local leader development processes to engage. Discussing accountability or responsibility in general without specific context is a start. But this is a topic particularly well suited to discussions with local commanders and staff so that examples can give specificity to concepts. The following is an example of intended empowerment that raised several issues:

Once Upon a Time, Long, Long Ago ...

... we were trying to train as we would fight and push decision-making to levels suitable for battle. It seemed logical that junior commanders should decide if it was necessary to have medical support at all live-fire events. There were two pertinent assumptions here: soldiers are trained in basic lifesaving techniques, and in battle we do not have ambulances following every squad or platoon.

Our newly announced rule was, "No medics are required on the firing range unless the unit commander feels otherwise." Make the decision based on the situation: if you are experimenting with emplacing new explosive charges in the middle of the night, maybe you should arrange for have a mobile surgical hospital to be handy; if you have an experienced unit on a rifle range within two minutes of the hospital, medics would seem unnecessary. The complete written guidance was, "Commanders will provide whatever medical or other support [on ranges] they determine necessary based on the type of exercise, the state of training of their soldiers, the availability of LIFESAVER aircraft [medical evacuation helicopters], and the location of the range. Routine presence of dedicated medical vehicles and aidmen on all standard ranges is not encouraged."

The usual range medical package had been two corpsmen with a small ambulance and a stack of reading material. Placing the responsibility at lower levels would replicate requirements in a combat situation and hopefully ease the mental transfer from garrison to battle mode. This policy, it was hoped, might also free up some medics to help at sick call and in the hospital wards, but that modest ancillary benefit did not dictate the new policy. We had been talking with commanders and staff for months about moving decisions downward to appropriate levels. Obviously, we had not been talking about it enough.

Commanders are responsible for everything their command does or fails to do. Army Regulation 600-20, November 6, 2014

126

Visiting a pistol range on a pleasant morning several weeks after the policy change had been announced, I asked the NCO in charge where the medics were. (There had not been a serious injury on that pistol range in fifty years. A great hospital was close by.) Now, I admit that mine was a leading question. He said, "General, the medics are over there behind that shed."

I said, "Why are they behind the shed?"

"Because if you had said, 'I don't see any medics and that is okay,' I would not have mentioned it. But if you asked, 'Where are the medics?' We've got 'em!"

Clearly, we had to regroup. Our new policy was not working. It was not working partly because subordinate leaders were not sure why we were doing it, and partly because they were not certain I would back their decision in case an accident happened that might have been less serious had an ambulance with medics been on hand. It was also a fear of change from old habits they had grown up with. It led to teaching sessions that I should have conducted well before we implemented the new policy.

As I recall, the "no medics unless it made sense" edict eventually took hold in just a few units on the post. Not surprisingly those units had other innovations that were also blossoming. Their commanders fit my biases about innovative leaders. But overall the new policy made too many people uncomfortable. Maybe it was not a good idea even if the intent were wholesome. They might have trusted me with their lives in combat, but not their careers in peacetime.

Note

21

Assessing Power Distribution and Trust

It is difficult to fix a dysfunctional situation—or celebrate a healthy one—if we cannot measure status and trends. The issues of centralization, empowerment, and respecting subordinate authority are not commonly analyzed. Perceived lack of authority and latitude to do the assigned job is a major complaint of leaders military and civilian.

The Assessment of Power Distribution in Organizations (APDO) instrument was designed for use in our Systems Leadership Program at CCL. (You can find it in Appendix A.) The version that follows is a slight adaptation. This instrument offers an innovative approach to determining perceptions of decentralization and trust. Those perceptions are strong elements in determining the success of any empowerment or mission-type order philosophy.

While the survey is a bit complex to administer, it offers unique quantitative insights. It requires the participation of three levels in the organization—boss, direct subordinates, and subordinates of those subordinates. Going two echelons down is necessary to determine if policies are understood and ongoing deeper into the system. The survey asks not only how the individual leader perceives the level of trust and empowerment but also asks the boss to predict the responses of subordinates and asks subordinates to predict the response of the boss—a Predicted Results Comparison (PRC) protocol.

This PRC or "what I think the other guy will say" technique stimulates discussion. For example, a brigade commander would take the survey, record his view of the climate, and predict how his subordinate lieutenant colonels would view the climate. Then the lieutenant colonels would do the same, predicting how both their boss and their subordinates (company commanders in this case) view the climate. Staff officers could also participate. Then the company commanders would record their view of the climate and how they believe their boss would assess the climate. The instruction for using the instrument must include identification of the "organization" we are talking about: battalion, brigade, staff section, installation, etc.

The survey also asks for two responses to each item: the strength of agreement with the statement, and how important that statement is in creating a healthy climate. All of the recorded perceptions would be displayed graphically, with proper attention to individual anonymity. The perceived levels of empowerment and the relative importance of each item—plus the differences in perception at different organizational echelons—would be displayed. In the case of empowerment or decentralization, perception is a major part of reality: "I have the authority and latitude to do my job or I do not."

Even if the boss's intentions are good, only the results as seen from the working level count. (Part 2 of the survey shown on Chart 4 most directly captures the state of empowerment.) Just discussing each of the items in the instrument and their relevance to the local situation is fodder for a stimulating multi-echelon discussion.

For the executives who used the APDO instrument in a leader development setting at CCL, it brought new insights. It was for most participants their first effort to quantify this aspect of organizational dynamics. It is most suited for brigade and division levels, but works also at battalion level and in staffs at division or higher. Here are sample items from the Assessment of Power Distribution in Organizations survey instrument:

Chart 4 Excerpts from the APDO Instrument

Item	Agreement	Importance
Our leaders trust subordinates and expect them to use good judgment. (People are treated as trustworthy and responsible adults.)		
Our leaders show their intent to empower subordinates and solve problems at the lowest possible level. (They know they cannot do it all.)		
Our higher headquarters understands that too many rules hamper necessary initiative. (They understand local initiative must be protected.)		
We have authority to make decisions at our level, and our leaders will back us up. (Our leaders don't interfere without good reason.)		
Our organization is serious about honesty and integrity. (We don't tolerate cheating by anybody for any purpose.)		
Our leaders typically solicit input before changing the rules of the game. (We are consulted when possible about matters in our area of expertise.)		
Developing subordinates—coaching and ensuring training—receives attention in our unit. (We get regular feedback and go to school on time.)		

Here is an example of results from 248 executives, military and civilian, who had their subordinates complete the survey. Such organizational data deserve further analysis to reveal meaning, significance, and any policy implications. All good surveys stimulate discussion.

The bosses saw these two items as significantly *more important* than did subordinates:

- Our organization is serious about honesty and integrity.
- Our senior leaders exemplify the espoused values of the organization.

In these two items, bosses' views were significantly *more positive* than subordinate views:

- Our leaders understand that inherently good programs may have disastrous side effects.
- Our leaders typically solicit input before changing the rules of the game.

The value of these comparative views comes from further discussion. What is the reason for the differing perspectives? Hierarchical position alone can lead to different views of operational priorities, openness of communications, fairness of policies, approachability of senior leaders, and even general health of the climate.

Note

22

Respecting the Authority and Responsibility of Subordinate Leaders

The need for respecting and protecting subordinate authority and turf in order to create a high-performing organization is rarely discussed in doctrine. *Decentralization* and *micromanagement* and *bypassing the chain of command* are not strongpoints in formal pronouncements, although sensitivity to the issues themselves is on the increase in high places. While doctrine and tradition speak to respecting the office and persona of seniors, *protecting subordinate authority* or *respecting subordinate turf* are not on the front line in rules and regulations. With the exception of those few prerogatives reserved to subordinate commanders by military law, and reminders in leadership texts to avoid micromanagement, doctrinal guidelines constraining downward incursions are weak. Adding *respect for subordinate authority* to our lexicon might enhance institutional awareness of the costs and dangers of meddling into subordinate business. Such awareness seems a treasured characteristic among commanders highly regarded by their subordinates.

The idea is not that the senior commander should be restricted from entering a subordinate domain. Leaders need to roam the battlefield, check the warehouse, visit the ammunition holding area, listen to discussions in the classroom, and sit in on planning conferences. Respecting subordinate authority—while simultaneously showing trust-- can be as simple as not being at the line of departure or avoiding the rail-loading operation or not soaring above the battle injecting advice. We might define respecting subordinate authority as "avoiding intrusion into the proper activities or prerogatives of subordinates in line or staff operations." The *or staff* is not a trivial element in the equation.

These admonitions or rules would not preclude any commander from inspecting, over-watching, guiding, surprising, firing, or directing from chopper or desk. We need to talk more regularly and specifically about the difference between healthy supervision and oppressive micromanagement. A suitable topic for unit leadership development seminars if the climate is right, it is an essential component of military school curricula-- replete with war stories and case studies of how leaders at both ends of the competence spectrum handled the issue.

The astute organizational scholar George Reed likes to remind that commanders have the right to select certain aspects of their operation for special scrutiny. As a major general in command of a division, I visited tank gunnery ranges. Sometime I would ride on the back deck and plug in to the intercom as the crew went through an already stressful exercise. This was my swooping far down, jumping about four echelons of command. But I wanted to get a feel for competence and commitment at the very tip of the spear, even as I believed in the competence and candor of my commanders.

We had worked hard at developing a command climate that would let me engage at lower levels without suggesting distrust or compromising authority. It can be done if the senior leader listens well, knows what he is looking for, refrains from giving guidance except to the commanders themselves—and then in private-- and treads lightly. Subordinates do not expect perfect behavior from the boss, with added latitude given if trust and open communication reside.

Examples of Intrusion into Subordinate Domains

Decentralization, empowerment, and the proper use of command authority deserve additional attention in schools and pre-command courses. Possible case study scenarios:

- A senior general declares that only a general officer may relieve a company commander. While this might introduce an added degree of fairness or consistency to the process, it also implies that intervening brigade and battalion commanders do not have the judgment to make such calls. What set of current circumstances or prior experiences might lead a general officer to make such a decision? What are the possible short-term and more enduring outcomes of such decisions on the climate and the culture?

- An installation policy requires a brigade-level commander to approve a leave longer than fifteen days. But the best judge of who can be spared and who deserves a leave is clearly the company-level commander. (That is, by the way, the same company commander who last week was entrusted with the lives of two hundred soldiers in freeing a village and reestablishing its government and fixing its water supply.) How do we determine at what level such specific personnel decisions should be made? What latitude should local commanders have in determining where authority levels reside? What criteria should commanders use as a guide in deciding which decisions to reserve for themselves?

- A local policy requires a commissioned officer as a range safety officer when in fact available senior noncommissioned officers are qualified for the assignment and the battalion or company commander in charge knows who they are. What should the criteria be for delegating particular tasks to particular grade levels? Who should develop such criteria? What routine processes should be in place to question current policies?

- Unit leader development programs, such as "sergeants' time," can become swamped by administration. Lesson plans and rehearsals not only wring the spontaneity and flexibility out of the program but also can turn a pleasant opportunity into an onerous drill. What particular phenomenon in the environment drives rather informal, low-maintenance programs into highly structured processes?

- Speeches to mass audiences have their place in leadership. Everybody wants to hear the news from the horse's mouth. When the commander-in-chief, service secretary, or service chief broadcasts to the troops it can be an uplifting and clarifying, not undermining anybody's authority. When the brigade commander has an inspiring message to deliver to the assembled troops, that might be worth the cost. Routine announcements of policy in mass formation, however, have high potential for damage. While administratively convenient, they bypass and weaken leaders' role as the primary conduit for organizational information. What are sensible guidelines here? Policies and plans passed down through the chain of command strengthen it. When the platoon leader and platoon sergeant hear the news the same time their troops do, that may be a lost opportunity to reinforce authority. How do we best communicate non-tactical, nonemergency information to the troops about new directives on physical training standards, new guidelines on wearing the uniform, or a change in unit deployment date?

- Unit coherence and leader sense of responsibility are enhanced by minimizing training by committee and maximizing training by members of the chain of command. One expert explaining to the massed battalion or company how to activate the new encryption device or strip the new machine gun should be a last resort. Instead, leaders should be trained by the expert so they can reinforce their authority by demonstrating their expertise. What are the criteria for determining whether subject-matter experts or members of the local chain of command conduct training?

- At every opportunity, pass the baton to the lowest unit that can execute. Do things by unit, not by roster. A conspicuous opportunity is morning PT. (By the way, why do we start it at 0600 or 0630 in garrison? This probably began in early

The general should often be present to praise some, to criticize others, and see with his own eyes that the orders … are observed exactly. Frederick the Great, 1747

WWII when time was of the essence and all soldiers--mostly unmarried--lived close by in barracks. To meet an 0630 formation today, some one-car family a few miles away got the baby up at 0530 to deliver the soldier. We once at our installation moved the voluntary start time to 0700. The sky did not fall. A few battalion-level leaders complained about cutting into maintenance time. But I digress.) While a battalion two-mile run now and then probably has merit (we did it for years in boots before running shoes were invented and thoughtfully authorized), this is a splendid opportunity to let platoon or even squad/section leaders take charge, instruct, set the example, and use initiative in creating a challenging, team-building event. They of course would also be responsible for their troops passing the PT test. Some organizations do it that way. Others still have mass formations with everybody in the same color shoestrings.

The idea of shielding subordinates from nonsense has been around for a long time. That in itself says something about our institution! Here are extracts from a post WW II letter written by the famed Tony McAuliffe--who replied "Nuts" to the German suggestion to surrender while surrounded at Bastogne in the winter of 1944. It was addressed to his subordinate general officer commanders when he was a lieutenant general commanding the Seventh Army in 1954:

> I desire by this letter to express certain of my thoughts upon an urgent and vexing problem which faces both the United States Army as a whole and our command in particular ... too often the junior officer and the senior non-commissioned officer ... consider their lots neither happy nor professionally stimulating ... a pronounced contract to the attitude existing prior to WW II.
>
> To improve this state of affairs, we must give emphasis to the decentralization of command, a departure from present practice ... A policy of decentralization infers a confidence by the senior in the junior ...

In the matter of training, all higher headquarters must seek to cut to a proper minimum the required hours for specified subjects … to leave to the company or battery commander reasonable latitude in the training of his unit … In training, it is necessary also to avoid over supervision. Battalion, regimental, or higher commanders should spend time in the field checking training, but company commanders must feel they are being trusted with the training of his company.

Another productive policy is that platoon leaders shall have totally unsupervised control of their platoons in the field for a twenty-four-hour period several times annually in training and if reasonable on operations as well. There is no objection to the company or battalion commander specifying in part what should be accomplished in the twenty-four hours, but the platoon should not be inspected or visited in this period of time. The platoon leader … will learn much from this experience …

A copy of this letter was sent by the army chief of staff to all general officers sometime in the 1970s. Like crabgrass, the over-supervision mode regenerates.

Once Upon a Time, Long, Long Ago …

… a retired friend doing some research on command climates and I strolled into one of the many motor pools on the base filled with the then-new M1 (Abrams) tanks. We were adjusting to their greatly enhanced capability. A sixty-ton battle machine that could shoot reliably on the move and race at unbelievable speeds over bumpy ground.

> I think we are over-centralized, overly bureaucratic, and overly risk-averse. General Mark Milley, Army Chief of Staff, 4 May, 2017.

Some of the local "ground" included clay. When mixed with the right amount of moisture it turned into a sticky mass that morphed to the consistency of titanium. And it collected under the fender-like cover of the drive sprockets. That hard-packed mud was so formidable it sometimes forced the track off the sprocket. That meant track replacement, a heavy, heavy task unloved by tankers.

As we were walking down a line of tanks, there was a small cluster of soldiers around the rear of one vehicle—probably a maintenance warrant officer and two or three sergeant mechanics and the tank commander. We eased up into the group as best a commanding general can ease up and asked how things were going and what the issue of the moment was. Well, the issue was what to do to about the mud being caught between the hull and the fender that was causing tracks to be thrown.

We all stood around for a couple minutes gazing at the fender shielding the final drive sprocket. It was designed to keep mud from being tossed in the air, with probably an additional role in reducing the tank's heat signature.

After a short period of contemplation, I said, "You know, if we were to cut a small oval section out of that fender, big enough to let some mud drop down but not so big as to expose the entire drive sprocket, maybe that would work."

They listened and nodded thankfully. We said goodbye and continued our walk. When out of hearing range but still in sight, my friend said, "Take a look at what's happening back there." I looked back and saw that the group had sort of dispersed.

"Boy, did you screw that up big time!" he said. "How in hell can they propose any other fix after you just made a command decision?"

I replied, "I didn't make a decision. I made a suggestion!"

He said, "You're kidding!"

He was, of course, right. I had screwed up. I had interfered with a small group of unit experts whose collective technical savvy exceeded mine. My suggestion had sucked some of the creative energy out of that part of our system.

Forging the Bottom of the Chain

At company level, with authority more fragile and personality-dependent than at higher echelons, seemingly benign policies can have enormous impact on leader authority and effectiveness. Institutions must continuously support junior leaders by policy as well as pronouncement. If leaders were provided the latitude and backing appropriate to their positions, and held accountable for high standards of unit performance, poor discipline and malfunctioning weapons would be rare—as they are in high-performing units. No junior leader problems would be headlined as part of a Joint Chiefs of Staff agenda. There would be no need to establish an ultimately dysfunctional if immediately comforting ad hoc stovepipe parallel bureaucracy to "help" commanders by bypassing them.

Removing traditional authority from junior commanders is the ultimate institutional distrust. That solution will never solve fundamental problems. Arms room weapons maintenance, range control protocols, equipment turn-in procedures, attending to misbehavior, and recognizing junior leader initiative all provide convenient opportunities to reinforce or undermine trust and accountability at unit level. Their prescribed disposition and resolution are in fact issues of strategic institutional importance. Few above company level ever pull a trigger.

Deciding who is responsible for the cleanliness of weapons stored in the arms room, or for supervising return of personal equipment to government control, or protecting the new soldier from hazing is critical to ensuring the strength of the chain at the tip of the spear. It also reflects understanding or lack thereof about organizational dynamics and the magic of conspicuous and accepted accountability for results. Seemingly innocuous policies in military organizations for ammunition accounting, vehicle dispatch, pushup counting, and proper wearing of the uniform remain specific opportunities for reinforcing subordinate authority and sense of responsibility. We hold leaders at all levels responsible for both process (hours and procedures for marksmanship training) and for outcomes (number of target hits.) This is, of course, something everybody already knows—but can somehow be forgotten now and then.

Chain of command responsibility can be gently but firmly undermined by such seemingly benign procedures as letting range control or some similar off-line activity take charge of an events under the guise of standardization or safety. While the administrative cadre on a firing range may be needed to coordinate start times and define safe firing areas, they have no business in unit discipline. For example, names or initials of individuals from the participating unit who may be in charge at the moment should never be revealed to the custodian of the range. Just the name of the unit will allow finding the commander who retains responsibility for all his unit does or does not do.

If there is a crew whose performance is notably weak—or worse—the chain of command, not the unit technical expert, should be held accountable. The master gunner or training officer or simulator controller, valuable as these individuals may be, should not be held directly responsible for operational effectiveness. The squad or section leader, not the arms-room keeper, is responsible for keeping weapons clean.

There should never be administrative chores and deadlines—such as daily reports by computer of training activities in progress—that prevent a leader from attending to important operational or training needs. Why this continues in some organizations is more than an interesting question. It may indicate that higher commanders are simply out of touch with the realities at company and battalion level, unaware of how much energy is being diverted from primary chores by reporting demands. Should laptops be prohibited below battalion level for anything but fire-control or navigation? Or mandatorily shut down at the end of the training day?

Note

24

Inspecting the Inspectors

Systems of regular inspections to assess compliance with standards, review use of resources, and evaluate the command climate are essential. However, there must be some semblance of balance of power between the mighty team of inspectors and the often seemingly powerless unit commanders. If not, the natural tension between the two compromises opportunities for constructive teaching and reliable status reporting. Left unattended, the inspectors will prevail in all arguments. So as part of any plan to sustain rational and motivational climates and appropriately distribute authority, inspection teams themselves need to be inspected.

A brief questionnaire about inspecting team behavior, developed jointly by unit commanders and the staff agencies sponsoring the inspection, can be a teaching tool for both parties. Such questionnaires offer an opportunity for inspected unit commanders to send their views to the boss, to whom the inspectors already have quick access to tell their version of the story.

Immediately after an inspection, the inspected unit commander completes the brief paper and pencil or electronic handheld survey, discusses it—or not—with the chief of the inspection team, and sends it to the commander who sponsored the inspection. Experience with this technique shows it can facilitate communication, build mutual trust, enhance the effectiveness of the inspection, and also counter any complaint by unit commanders that only the inspectors get to be heard.

Inspection checklists trump command-articulated policies hands down. Inspections and reports are principal determinants of behavior, whether we like it or not. This persists even in strong, healthy units led by thoughtful commanders.

Once Upon a Time, Long, Long Ago …

… I was casually—at least casually in my mind--visiting an almost abandoned concrete warehouse. (It was a slow day.) The huge facility, built to store WWII munitions, was now used for general storage. It was a gigantic domed structure open at each end; you could drive four trucks abreast through it.

I noticed a corporal taping a sign to the concrete wall. His sign had a rectangle representing the building and arrows pointing to the open ends. Sure enough, it was the prototypical fire evacuation diagram. I asked, "Corporal, what are you doing?"

He said, "General, I am putting up a fire evacuation diagram."

I said, "But this is a concrete building open at both ends! What's the purpose of a fire evacuation diagram in here?"

He said, "General, it doesn't have a purpose. It's for inspection!"

Just then, his lieutenant arrived and said, "Sir, I heard about your policy about useless fire evacuation diagrams. But we have an inspection tomorrow. And you never know what the inspectors will want!"

Yep, inspections win over both pronouncements of command policy and common sense. It's not even close. Things that get counted and reported draw attention. Once again, I had failed to explain to the fire marshal and his loyal band of inspectors, as well as to my unit commanders, that we were against nonsense and that I expected everybody to apply that guidance ruthlessly.

Here is an example of the Inspect the Inspector report. It received good marks from both unit commanders and inspectors. As I recall, just one or two inspectors were fired over a period of three years as unable to relate to unit commanders. They had repeatedly forgotten the purpose of the exercise.

Comments about the inspecting teams were usually favorable. And unit commanders no longer saw themselves as impotent in any contest with outside examiners. Completing the report took about five minutes. There was no need for endorsement, duplication, uploading, or filing. Just send it to the commander for whom the inspectors work.

Chart 5 Inspect the Inspector

Inspect the Inspector Program: Unit Commander's Comments on the Inspection			
Unit: Date:			
Announced? Y N Requested? Y N			
1. Findings of the inspection team the unit commander considers significant:			
2. Findings of the inspection team the unit commander considers trivial or inappropriate:			
3. Unit commander's comments on the inspection or visit			
	Yes	No	Notes and comments
a. Appropriately comprehensive?			
b. Attention to important items?			
c. Fair, impartial, objective evaluation?			
d. Consistent with published standards?			
e. Evaluations consistent with prior visits?			
f. Feedback, coaching provided to the unit?			

Note

25

The Policy Quiz

Policies and their updates often escape coordination and clarification. The policy quiz instrument is a provocative, usually enjoyable method of determining if policies are understood where the rubber meets the road. It is an early step toward "finding out what is going on around here" in the master plan for crafting a coherent environment.

Developing simple true-false questions for the instrument is a productive beginning of the exercise. That process allows commanders and staffs to review and agree on a brief statement about selected policies. Just that effort can be surprisingly educational for all parties. Ambiguity can slip into policies from multiple directions. Too often, a commander's casual remark or attempted clarification by a well-meaning assistant is the culprit. These de facto modifications are often unbeknown to the primary staff or the commander. It is not a trivial exercise for any headquarters to agree on what are its policies and their intent even before determining if they have been transmitted with high fidelity to the working level.

After the quiz has been designed, it deserves field trials to see if it makes sense to the prospective participants, such as junior subordinate commanders or first sergeants. Some of them should have contributed to its initial design. After that vetting and appropriate modification, the participants—best in small groups—complete the short (one page, maybe twenty questions, less than ten minutes) true-false Policy Quiz.

Here are two sample questions. They are basic in construct, but their interpretation and application can reveal a great deal about culture and communication.

- "It is Corps [could be battalion or unit] policy that an NCO in the grade of E-7 or higher must accompany a departing soldier to the TA-50 turn-in point."

  Answer: False. Not our policy. Let company commanders decide. Don't waste NCO time. Don't imply our soldiers can't reliably turn in their gear. But do keep an eye on how the policy is working.

- "It is Corps policy that soldiers should have at least seven days' notice before a change in the training/operations schedule."

  Answer: True. (Obviously excluding alerts and no-notice exercises.) There needs to be thoughtful analysis of the practicability of this noble intention. (I am not familiar with any organization—including mine--that made it work, although some statistics said it did.) Lack of advance notice falls mostly on the back of the junior leaders and soldiers—and their families. It is probably a reflection of a high mission-to-resource ratio, a can-do attitude, personnel turbulence, and in some cases just a flat lack of understanding about life at company level.

At the first use of the policy quiz on our post in 1981, two dozen company commanders and first sergeants together in one room took our five-minute twenty-question true-or-false version. The results were interesting to all, startling to some. Some of the commander's favorite policies, so clear and precious to everybody at headquarters, did not travel well through the bureaucratic gauntlet to where the action is. Few attendees got more than 80 percent of the true-false items correct. This produced some institutionally-strategic insights.

The discussions that followed about the correct answers, the intent of the policies, and why some of them made or no longer made sense were worth the price of admission. Some policies needed more than just a better articulation—they needed substantive modification. Since the senior commander was present, such actions could be expedited.

They could be even better "expedited" if some staff officers had been present to take notes. There might have been some additional trust in the system's responsiveness and rationality as a result of the exercise.

The quiz can be a productive also as a teaching tool at regular command and staff sessions, both in garrison and in the field. Topics for such quiz in an operational environment might include policies on rules of engagement, handling of cash, medical evacuation, and turn-in of equipment. The process can be a team-building exercise in any environment, just as an after-action review can be.

Having staff officers from the directing headquarters sit in on the debrief brings additional payoff. There is nothing better to make a staff officer feel part of the team than to participate in an exercise like this—even if they find that their favorite policy is not a jewel from a subordinate commander's perspective.

Here are a few other items that might be used in a division setting, this version including both garrison and field items. The third and fourth columns that permit rating the policy itself as good or dumb can be added for additional fun. If the climate is open, a compilation and display of the good versus dumb responses can initiate another productive discussion, reinforcing the theme of uninhibited exchange of viewpoints. Naturally, the commander has the final say.

Dumb stuff is particularly galling to soldiers who have spent considerable time in war. As Dr. Tim Kane notes in a recent paper on fiscal and motivational aspects of our volunteer Army, "American troops are coming home with little tolerance for regulatory barriers to excellence."[49]

---

[49] Kane 2017, 56.

Chart 6 The Policy Quiz

#	Our Policy: True or False? Good or Dumb Policy?	True	False	Good	Dumb
1.	Every soldier will take a PT test semiannually unless medically excused.				
2.	Field exercise deployments will never start on Monday.				
3.	Full body armor will be worn when "outside the wire."				
4.	Changes in schedules less than seven days ahead require O-6 approval.				
5.	Live ammo held overnight at base camp must be under armed guard.				
6.	"Sergeants' time" schedules must be approved by brigade HQ.				
7.	Live fire ranges must be supervised by a certified O-3 or higher leader.				
+					
+					

Notes from the Notes of Part 5

PART 5

Organizational Climates and Trust

It is not enough to fight. It is the spirit which we bring that decides the issue. It is morale that wins the victory.

General George C. Marshall

Note 26

Leaders and Command Climates

Creating a healthy climate is the most important long-term task of a leader. It is a major responsibility at all levels, but especially at battalion on up. The most reliable measure of a commander's sustained performance is the health of the resulting climate. (Spectacularly good surveys for climate analysis, available for free, are included in Notes 27 and 28 and in Appendix A.)

Climate and culture are similar but different animals. *Climate* is basically how individuals feel about the organization: "My work is important and satisfying. I am challenged and appreciated." *Culture* is basically how we do things around here: "Everybody in this outfit carries his share of the load" or "We are always professionals." Climate is obviously a more temporary, malleable state of morale. Culture reflects institutional values, customs, and shared expectations about correct behavior.

Our discussion in these Notes is mostly about climates—in the civilian world, "organizational climates" or "what energizes us at work," and in the military world, "command or staff climates." There is academic discourse about what size organizational entity can have an identifiable (homogeneous, distinctive) climate. No doubt that a company (a military unit of perhaps one hundred to two hundred people, divided into three to five platoons or sections) has one of its own. Maybe a platoon does too, but that climate is more likely a limb of the company. A battalion (three to six companies normally) has a climate, even though individual company climates may differ based on the styles of their commanders.

Staffs of battalions and higher organizations often have a distinct climate within their parent organization. This is particularly true at higher levels where staffs are major entities of dozens or hundreds of individuals, often with major differences in climate among the various sub-directorates. At higher levels—division, corps, and installation—the concept of a discernible, homogeneous climate is a bit squishy. Still, there are often palpable if not distinct differences among brigades and divisions and posts.

The condition of climates among larger entities is often revealed by a general perception of whether or not "things make sense around here." (Camp Swampy is: a. "a good place to serve" or b. "to be avoided at all costs.")

The Power of Local Commanders

How the culture of the institution has been transformed, for better or worse, by local command policies plays a critical role in the quality of the climate. One of the interesting conclusions, after collecting survey data from a variety of organizations of the same type, mission, and resources, is the discernible difference in soldier attitudes, confidence, and enthusiasm that can only come from variance in local leadership. Again, the battalion-level commander has enormous impact.

Naturally, institutional policies, the budget, the weather, and the price of oil all come into play. But morale, retention, and other offshoots of organizational climates remain more the offspring of local leadership than of any other variable. The most direct way any institution could retain more of its outstanding junior leaders would be to more carefully select and prepare leaders for battalion-level command or its equivalent.

> The commander is responsible for establishing the leadership climate of the unit and developing disciplined and cohesive units. Army Regulation 600-20, November 6, 2014

Processes for more thorough examination of past performance and future potential during the selection process for command are available. They are time-consuming, expensive, and necessary. A few are in place: some having evolved from creative practices of local commanders, some from innovations from on high. Examinations of cognitive competence, screening for emotional health, and analysis of resilience and empathy can add unique insights to traditional performance data almost exclusively generated from top-down assessments.

Contemporary personnel records are somewhat thin in useful discussion of strengths and weaknesses when it is time to select officers for battalion command level. A possible and understandably controversial approach toward greater assurance of competence in command at this level would be to make the first six months probationary. After six months, a comprehensive review, designed using a variety of assessment tools along with senior commander evaluations, would determine fitness to continue in command. Yes, unless very carefully executed--perhaps even then--it would bring added stress to that first six months.

The benefit of any doubt regarding suitability as a commander—not as an officer but as a commander—should go to the needs of the institution instead of the individual. This might be contrary to what is fashionable in the world of human resources, but such decisions carry enormous implications for long-term force competence. Officers who did not survive the probationary period would not automatically be denied options for future promotion.

Taking the Pulse of the Organization

Unhappy people are less productive over time. Research is clear on this point. While happiness does not guarantee productivity—there are happy, incompetent organizations—things being anywhere near equal, happy people (meaning energized, trusted, challenged, and focused) do better in war and peace by every measure.

Experienced leaders can sense how their troops feel. Walking around and sensing the mood is well worth the time. However, there is no substitute for a properly designed and administered survey to find out what is going on in enough detail to reinforce success or fix failure. In most cultures, not taking advantage of the data to reinforce success is the more common sin. It is worth noting also that undigested climate data can be a ripe opportunity for nitpicking and second-guessing—another reason for leaders to have more than a fleeting relationship with how to use climate surveys.

Many of the techniques needed to create a suitable environment in which leaders can lead require an understanding of how organizations work-- how their policies interact, possibly conflict, can be misinterpreted, and modify the climate. These leaders need be alert for subtle second- and third-order effects. Such well-intentioned policies as detailed prescriptions for use of local funds, restrictions on assignments of junior leaders, mandatory coaching sessions, reports on completion of mandatory orientations, small arms security, or prizes to units based on quantity of achievements could generate unforeseen side effects.

There is more exciting information on climates and surveys in Notes 27, 28, and 29.

> No man can justly be called a great captain who does not know how to organize and forge the character of an army. Sir William Napier[50]

---

[50] Sir William Napier, 1785–1860, was a general with a distinguished combat record and a noted historian.

Powerful, Measurable Components of a Climate

Get these first three right and things in the organization cannot go far wrong:

1. **An unimpeded flow of information in all directions.** Upward flow is a bear, but a steady, reliable downward flow is almost as tough. Because unimpeded flow depends on so many interrelated parts of both culture and climate, it singularly reveals more about overall health than any other element. It is an even better gauge of organizational health and discipline than clarity of goals or mutual trust. Its attainment depends on both of those powerful components.

2. **Clarity on goals, missions, standards, and priorities.** This is a primary concern in all organizations. It is close to open flow of information in importance, and the first thing a good leader will review as a potential source of any organizational dissonance. Clarifying and updating priorities is often neglected. Commanders and staffs sometimes change priorities without promptly informing all concerned parties.

3. **A prevailing sense of mutual trust and confidence.** Such a sense is essential for any kind of Mission Command or true empowerment. There must be trust in organizational leaders both near and far, but especially near. Trust in the institution itself is built upon confidence in the rationale and coherence of policies and their thoughtful administration. Trust in the local leader may be more immediately important than trust in the institution. Among other things,

the local leader can be a heat shield, translator, or ameliorator of complex or questionable policies.

Other major components of a healthy climate include the following:

4. **A clear and coherent focus on mission accomplishment.** A collective urge to accomplish the mission may be easier to generate than a real-time understanding of intermediate objectives and operational priorities. Coherence is greatly helped by explaining in as much detail as time permits the commander's intent.

5. **Consideration for the well-being of every individual in the organization.** The first act of consideration is to train individuals for their jobs so they can work as a team and win. Consideration also means giving them coherent guidance as well as suitable collective protection. There must be both a clear articulation of policies designed to generate respect for each individual and a convenient method for individuals to address grievances. Disciplinary action against those who misbehave also enhances individual well-being.

6. **A sense of fairness in policies and policy implementation.** What is "fair" to the institution is not always perceived as such by members of the cast. In healthy climates, the affected members participate in decision-making whenever practicable. Also, whenever time permits, the rationale for decisions is explained. Awards, promotions, and disciplinary actions are handled without discrimination.

7. **An appreciation for initiative and innovation.** Ideas are welcome. The messenger is never shot because of discouraging words. Honest mistakes from good intentions are understood. "That's the way we have always done it" is prohibited language.

8. **A confidence that adequate resources are, or will be, on hand to accomplish the assigned mission.** If there is in fact a need to execute a "mission near impossible," the troops can handle that as long as the leaders are straight with them about the situation.

9. **An opportunity for individuals to learn and grow as members of the profession.** There are both good intentions and resources provided for continuing education; leaders express an interest in subordinate growth; and there is coaching on how to learn from experience augmented by a method for passing on lessons learned to the next shift. "That may have been what they told you in school, but this is the way we always do it here" is also banned from the vocabulary.

A survey with the five key elements in the 2004 and 2010 studies can be found in Appendix A.

A More Definitive Climate Survey

Questions like these in a longer survey permit a more detailed review of specific components of the organizational climate. The full survey with its twenty-two questions and space for the local commander to insert items to address his particular interest can be found in Appendix A.

Chart 7 Climate Survey Sample Items

	Item	Evaluation
	We have high standards of discipline in this unit.	
	We have clear goals and priorities.	
	We have a lot of teamwork going on in this unit.	
	We have the resources we need to do our job properly.	
	Our leaders put mission first, their own careers second.	
	Leaders in this unit are open to new ideas.	
	If I have a … problem, I am comfortable asking for help.	

Note

28

Rules about Climate Surveys

Informed twenty-first-century leaders—not just the HR folks but the leaders—need to understand the potency, utility, and potential mischief of surveys. Survey participation influences perceptions of organizational values and competence. Survey results can influence policy decisions. They also consume organizational energy.

The face validity and processing efficiency of surveys can influence perceptions of institutional competence. There must be expectations of their utility and confidence in their validity to ensure participant candor. There needs to be useful, timely, coherent feedback generated from informed analysis of the data. Sometimes data drift off into someplace, never to be heard of again. Above all, there must be clear rules religiously followed about individual and unit confidentiality.

For a time years ago, commanders had handy the advice of an organizational effectiveness staff officer (OESO) to help with matters of organizational development. Over fifteen years, starting in the early 1970s, the Army trained about three thousand officers for this role. They advised commanders about concepts and tools for forming and assessing healthy climates. A decision to save or transfer personnel spaces terminated the OESO program.[51]

The need for insight and policies addressing the challenges of maintaining proper climates remains. The commander has to be an informed and active participant.

---

[51] Ricks, *The Generals,* 363. This well-researched book by an insightful observer provides a rare and rich background on various aspects of senior military leadership. The OESO decision remains questionable.

Guidelines for Climate and Other Surveys

1. The organizational commander and the participants need to know the purpose of the exercise, the time it will take to participate, and why they have been selected.

2. Because of the time surveys consume, the messages they deliver regarding institutional concerns and priorities, and their potential role in crafting policies, commanders should be familiar with the objective and the content of surveys completed in their units.

3. If the proposed survey instrument or protocol appears poorly designed, or if there is no real intent to take advantage of the data and give feedback to participants, take steps to abandon the whole thing. If mandatory, which headquarters can remove that mandate? (Also, a survey designed to capture one aspect of the climate, such as an Equal Opportunity or Drug and Alcohol Abuse, is not a suitable instrument for assessing the quality of the overall climate.)

4. The participants need to know who will see the results, how the results will be aggregated and presented, and when and which results will be available to them. They need to understand how individual input will be protected and not disclosed without their consent.

5. Every item on the survey should be vetted for common sense and clarity by peers of prospective participants.

6. Optimally, the survey should not take more than twenty minutes to complete after the orientation. One page is best. Scholars and computers argue for longer. The purpose and intention determines the proper length.

7. If at all possible, make time to carefully discuss the survey with the participants after its completion. (Often the reply to a suggestion for this follow-up is "We do not have the time." That response deserves further examination.) Ask about the relevance of the questions, their reasons for particular responses, the plans for future follow-up, etc. In the division commander studies, for example, small groups completed the survey and then spent a half hour or more with the survey

team discussing their responses. Discussions did not identify individual or team participants.

8. Somebody should be preserving the data—in a confidential and accessible format—to allow analysis of trends and to extract meaningful lessons useful in leader development programs. This is a relatively expensive task that pays off only in the future. It is therefore often postponed past the date when the data can be retrieved and archived properly.

Note

29

Monitoring Obstacles to a Productive Training Climate

The purpose of this exercise is to determine which policies or procedures are in fact creating a barrier to effective training in the eyes of junior commanders. Leaders at company and battalion level have the best view of the total impact of the many factors that facilitate or encumber effective training. This is another exercise that enhances communication.

A sample of company-level commanders was queried to get their perspectives on which activities or policies were inhibiting training. A brief survey was then developed based on their input. The draft survey and plans for use were discussed with battalion and higher commanders and staff officers to keep them in the loop. Distractors on the survey were identified as either local responsibility or the result of policies of higher headquarters. The discussion on whose headquarters was the primary source of the problem was useful in framing a larger perspective.

Each major command was required to have 50 percent of company-level commanders complete the survey quarterly (it took five minutes max). Summarizing results was easy.

After the first couple of iterations, three months apart, we moved to semiannual. Some items were considered fixed and deleted. A few new ones that had popped up were added. The results were tallied, published, and discussed at appropriate levels. The following is one example: (This approach can be as useful when deployed as in garrison. Maybe more so.)

Chart 8 Feedback on Training Distractors from Company-Level Commanders

Problem source	Distractor	Major issue	Minor issue	Non-issue	Now better	Now worse	No change
Higher	NCO shortages						
Higher	Repair parts delays						
Higher	Mandatory social training						
Local	Conflicting training priorities						
Local	Management of school quotas						
Local	Too many meetings						
Local	Inadequate time between events						
Local	Range scheduling bureaucracy						
Local	Paperwork I have to complete						
Local	Short notice on big events						
Local	Too many visitors from higher HQ						
Local	Too many reports like this one						
Local	Add a new one						

Eliminating Dumb Stuff

Eliminating dumb stuff from the workplace gives everything a boost. Serious support of "If it's dumb, it's not our policy!" enriches life at every echelon. But who defines *dumb*? How does the commander learn that there are concerns about dumb stuff? How do we support disciplined response to policies while encouraging feedback about apparently dysfunctional ones?

Commanders master today's mission, plan for tomorrow, fine-tune policies, investigate any disruptions, reinforce trust, and take advantage of new ideas all at the same time. Part of the work includes bringing coherence and rationality into the climate through clearing at least part of the administrative jungle. Periodic junk-destruction campaigns are essential. Like crabgrass, administrative clutter and dumb stuff in general cling to life and sprout next year.

Clearing an administrative jungle is tough business for even the experienced, confident commander. Most policies, rules, and regulations had some semblance of justification at their birth. Their sponsors had good intentions, even if those intentions were shortsighted or strategically uninformed.

Once Upon a Time, Long, Long Ago …

… at the end of the Korean War, our unit was camped on a beach several miles back of the front lines. We slept in vehicles and tents. It was relatively peaceful. One night on an exercise in a heavy rain a soldier lost his weapon—or maybe it was dropped in the sand and run over by a truck. I can't remember for sure.

A lost weapon is never taken lightly. The local investigation concluded that the owner this time was not at fault. He should not have to pay for the weapon, even though he might have been disciplined for its loss.

Our unit reported to higher headquarters (in Japan!) our conclusion that reimbursement to the U.S. government was not warranted. We explained why. About two weeks later, we received the decision that the soldier absolutely must pay for that weapon. I remember the words of explanation exactly: "A prudent soldier would have kept his weapon in a locked wall locker!"

We didn't have many wall lockers, lockable or not. That headquarters was in a different world. As I found in future campaigns, it doesn't take much geographic distance behind the front to have a dramatically different view of life.

Some Specifics on Eliminating Dumb Stuff

Eliminating dumb stuff in garrison also sets the stage for logical policies in field operations. The commander needs to explain the rule that "If it's dumb, it's not our policy!" The commander needs to explain the criteria for dumb—and listen for ideas on the subject—realizing that what is dumb at one echelon may make sense at another. There needs to be a common understanding of the criteria for dumb.

There needs also a convenient communication channel that lets subordinate individuals—and organizations—notify the headquarters about perceived dumb stuff. The headquarters needs a plan for reviewing input promptly and informing all parties of why the complaint is or is not valid, and how the system could or will be modified to "de-dumb" that item. The system can ask for the name of the author of the complaint or accept anonymous notes. Interestingly, when the option was for either anonymous or identifiable messages on a "report dumb line," the majority of messages included name and unit. This is an indicator of upward trust that can be reinforced or undermined by the quality and timeliness of the response to the suggestion.

The commander needs to get into the act at least initially, and to teach the staff and subordinate commanders how to decide on dumbness and how to craft a sensible response to queries. A staff reply to a query early in our experimentation of exploring about things seen as dumb was, "The reason we are doing that is because it is our policy!" Obviously, we had to engage in an educational program for our headquarters staff to improve the quality of our responses. That discussion was also productive.

A program to combat dumbness needs continuing fertilization or it will wither away. Somebody senior on the staff needs to be responsible for tracking trends in numbers and topics of queries, and the quality and timeliness of staff responses. Not a bad item to be included in quarterly progress or readiness briefings.

> Be strict in your discipline; that is, to require nothing unreasonable of your officers and men, but see that whatever is required be punctually complied with. Reward and praise every man according to his merit, without partiality or prejudice; hear his complaints; if well founded, redress them; if otherwise discourage them in order to prevent frivolous ones. General George Washington

Notes from the Notes of Part 5

PART 6

Managing Organizations and Leading Staffs

Now there are five matters to which a general must pay strict heed. The first of these is administration; the second, preparedness; the third, determination; the fourth prudence; and the fifth, economy.

Wu Qi,[52] 430 AD

---

[52] Wu Qi (or Wu Chi) wrote of the need for motivated, highly trained soldiers. As a successful general, he inspired his troops by sharing their hardships. Although mindful of his soldiers' needs and considerate of his organizations, he was also a likely murderer of family members.

Note
31

A Master Plan for Organizational Leadership

This plan to create a productive climate where leaders at all levels can lead was designed for use in an executive development program taught at the Center for Creative Leadership when I was its president. We titled the program "Systems Leadership." It received pretty good marks. About three-quarters of the participants in the four-day program were from the corporate world; the others were current or retired military. Preparing and teaching the program was another learning exercise.

We described systems leadership as "a process for developing highly productive organizations through the creative integration of all operating systems." In other words, it is a recipe for scanning the entire organization and responding with a systemic approach. It recognizes that everything is interconnected and that operations must be guided by organizational values. Conceptual tools for leading complex organizations include the reality that different levels have different responsibilities; that organizational climates are the product of leaders and leader policies that can be analyzed and modified; and that distribution of power (latitude and authority) in an organization deserves direct attention.

Systemic thinking as described in our ten items below is most applicable to organizations where the commander has some influence on personnel management and resource distribution. The basic concepts are useful at any level.

1. First, get in touch with what really is going on in the organization and what people at different levels in the organization think about key elements of the climate.

2. Spend time (continuously) articulating the vision and clarifying goals, standards, and priorities. Make it easy for individuals and teams to question whether or not a particular policy is consistent with expressed organizational values.

3. Develop a clear plan for creating and sustaining a climate that is routinely supportive, rational, trusting, open, and integrated. Drafting the plan should be a team effort.

   a. Ensure that the staff acts to reinforce the leader's intent and organization's vision and priorities through coordination and integration of policies and programs—and establish communication channels for uncovering disconnects and dysfunctions.

   b. Focus organizational energy on priority matters; attack nonproductive policies and meaningless routines. Keep some energy free for adaptation and innovation.

   c. Ensure that leaders do not routinely handle actions that could be done as well by subordinate leaders, and that latitude to act is described for each level. Describe the model of an empowered leader—the need for clear understanding of goals and priorities, authority, and responsibilities.

   d. Explain the intent of all directives and rules so that subordinates can use initiative and independent action to achieve the objective.

   e. Ensure that policy or procedural changes are explained first to intermediate leaders and supervisors so they may in turn explain to their subordinates the rationale for those changes.

4. Insist that key leaders set the example in representing the organization's values, vision, and priorities. Take prompt action when leaders do not. Ensure that leaders understand their role in trust-building.

5. Design carefully a system for periodically measuring and reporting organizational efficiency, effectiveness, and climate that clearly supports organizational goals, priorities, and quality standards.

6. Reinforce outstanding individual and team accomplishment with an appraisal and reward system whose rules are straightforward and open to discussion, and which is consistent with desired organizational values. Encourage risk-taking and trust-building while focusing on quality output.

7. Attend to personnel selection, development, and promotion so that these systems identify, motivate, and educate potential leaders.

8. Eliminate any competition that hampers idea-sharing or teamwork across the organization.

9. Assume good intent. When something goes wrong, check first for flaws in the system. Trust people but be suspicious of systems.

10. Plan for succession and transition of key leaders.

The Systems Leadership Report Card (SLRC) found in Appendix A solicits input about the processes designed to achieve the proper climate. Both military and corporate leaders have found it useful. (Note 28 described a less complex instrument designed to measure key elements of the climate.) Instruments like these can be powerful in articulating and reinforcing institutional priorities and stimulating discussions about reality.

Here are a few representative items from the SLRC. They cover major outcomes instead of desired behaviors found on other included instruments:

- value reinforcement (organizational values clarified and nourished routinely)
- goals and priorities (knowing clearly the performance goals and task priorities)

- team-building (cooperative group work routinely supported)
- junk destruction (opportunities to eliminate dumb stuff and whitewash)
- pace and stress (reasonable levels of activity and demands for the situation)
- policy coherence (policies and practices congruent with goals and priorities)
- personal development (plans and programs for growing future leaders)

Remember that war is always a far worse muddle than anything you can produce in peace, and that sorting out muddles is really the chief job of a commander and his staff … but find out afterward how that particular muddle occurred and, if possible, don't let it happen again. Sir A. P. Wavell,[53] 1933

---

[53] Sir Alexander P. Wavell, 1883–1950, was a student of warfare noted for efficient employment of his forces. His World War II performance as a field commander in very difficult circumstances received mixed reviews.

The Awesome Power of Measuring and Reporting

Measuring and reporting progress and status are the least appreciated aspects of organizational dynamics. They advertise institutional values, set standards, articulate and influence command priorities, affect careers, absorb enormous energy, and are an invitation to all kinds of micro and macro manipulation and misuse. Although they can be grand motivators of individuals and units, when unwisely designed or implemented they can become a source of unhealthy competition, wasted energy, faulty decisions, and ethical malpractice.

Most of us want to do good work. Few start the day determined to sabotage the operation. People want to succeed, compete, win, and be appreciated. If you don't believe that, you are not suited for the leadership business. We are additionally motivated by the realization of the criticality of the work and the need to support the team. Also pertinent are the need for acceptance from our peers, respect from our subordinates, and feedback on our performance.

We want ourselves and our unit to be fairly appraised and offered the opportunity to do even better next time. We want competitions to make sense and be fair, to have opportunities for learning, and to keep our environment safe from trivia and nonsense.

Measuring Efficiency and Effectiveness—Considerations and Concepts

Measuring things accurately is both an art and a science. The methods used have a powerful influence on operations and are de facto promulgators of command priorities. Measurement practices can be used to educate, motivate, and sensitize, as well as to reveal the status of comparative systems. Their reliability and effectiveness affects overall confidence in organizational communications and the sense of institutional competence.

Commanders need to generate quantitative data that supplement qualitative evaluations. The larger the organization, the more pressing the need to review status, trends, and causality. A commander's skill in measuring things—in understanding the process—is a major component of effectiveness and of reputation as a trusted leader.

Poorly designed measurement systems, cumbersome or unreliable, are major sources of frustration with bureaucracy. They can also trigger ethical dilemmas if impossible or trivial goals are imposed. How the results of measurement data are compiled, presented, and distributed is also a major consideration; all participants need to know the rules before the game starts. The process of measuring and reporting is so critical that the subject deserves a prime spot in the education of leaders.

The first step in the design of a measurement or reporting system is identifying its purpose as one of the following:

- to evaluate overall progress toward one or more organizational goals (example: percent of individuals qualified on their individual weapon—with attention to defining *qualified*)
- to evaluate the efficiency of a system (example: time to process a TDY claim)
- to evaluate the effectiveness of a program (example: weight loss after thirty days in the program)
- to compare the efficiency or effectiveness of one part of an organization with another (example: reenlistment rates, vehicle accidents, materiel downtime, equipment losses, foot and ankle injuries, self-inflicted wounds, DUI rates, etc.

Note that such comparisons have high potential for mischief unless the criteria are clear, the data collection reliable, and bosses aware the playing field must be level.)

- to compare the accomplishments of individuals in the organization against prescribed standards (example: PT test scores, weapons qualification.)
- to evaluate the adequacy of systems supporting the organization (example: time to process a medical discharge; time to fill a parts requisition; time between call for fire and first rounds on target; percentage of on-hand versus authorized chaplains.)

There are specific costs associated with measurement. *Objective costs* include manpower to design, administer, collect, organize, display, report, discuss, archive, and retrieve the data. *Subjective costs* reflect possible confusion regarding organizational priorities and philosophies: Do these measures and any goals represent current priorities? Do these measures support the concept of trust in subordinates? Will the commander understand their meaning and be aware of the environment in which they were captured? Does the commander use these data in such a manner as to create inappropriate competition or unproductive stress among subordinates?

The following questions regarding measurement and reporting should be discussed:

- What is the purpose of this measurement exercise? (See possible purposes above.)
- What is the expected accuracy, reliability, and comparability of the data? Are all variations in data over time under the control of reporting units? Are we measuring the same phenomenon at each reporting interval?
- Is there a potential for misinterpretation or misuse? How easy is it to jump to premature judgments from a quick look at the data? How difficult will it be to interpret and explain the significance of differences over time or among units?

- What is the bloat potential? How likely is it that the whole complexity of the process over time will grow into a real burden not worth the effort but with no sundown clause?

- What is the planned visibility at various levels? Who sees the data in what level of consolidation? (Brigade averages or individual brigade scores, identified or unidentified; top five platoons vs. bottom five, identified or unidentified; etc.)

- Are there opportunities for subordinates to suggest modification of the procedures? If commanders want to update, modify, or delete a reporting requirement, how do they suggest those changes?

- What is the interval and frequency of the report? Climates take a while to change, so anything less than a six-month interval between iterations of a survey would be questionable, while levels of artillery rounds at the local ammo point might be reported daily. (One commander I knew would take the gamble of not forwarding certain reports to see if anybody noticed. Sometimes nobody did!)

- How intrusive is the collection process? Measuring garbage after meals or oil filter use is one type; keeping scores at PT testing is another; evaluating the decision-making process in the TOC is another; and observing 360 feedback processes is still another. Each has varying burdens to produce, organize, and archive.

Once Upon a Time, Long, Long Ago …

… I had been in command of my second company for about three weeks when we received news that General Maxwell D. Taylor, the Theater CINC himself, would present us with an award. That award was for that tank company having gone an entire year with no reported venereal disease. VD was a big issue in post-WWII Japan. Statistics were compared, advertised, and discussed. My new command had 140 healthy tankers not far from a friendly little town filled with places of amusement. A full 365 days without a single case of VD—when comparable units were averaging 10 to 20 percent infected—was simply remarkable!

The big day came, and the four-star general and a cadre of colonels arrived at First Lieutenant Ulmer's company area. It had been cleaned up—gravel paths raked, latrines scrubbed, etc. Notably and pleasantly, I had not been heavily supervised by the battalion staff during our preparations. My carefully planned tour of the company area included leading the visiting party in single file through the front door of the dayroom to view our pool table, magazines, and blackboard.

We planned to walk down the narrow aisle between the folding chairs that made our dayroom into our classroom, straight out the back door at the other end of the room. We would walk out that door and back up the company street between the wooden buildings that had been home earlier to a Japanese Infantry unit.

Not wanting the troops to come into the spotless dayroom from the back door and mess it up, the first sergeant had locked that rear door shut earlier in the day. He had forgotten to unlock it. As I tried to open the door and could not, the line of generals and colonels behind me came to a halt. We had to turn around and retrace our steps, nudging each other in the crowded aisle back to the front door.

I remember the scowls on the faces of the general's staff as they were displeased by my obvious incompetence. Seeing their disgruntlement was somehow funny. But I also felt some anguish over my clumsy failure as host to a real dignitary.

The company formed up outside at attention. The award was presented by General Taylor. He appeared unruffled by the dayroom disaster; after all, he had clandestinely entered Italy by submarine and commanded the 101st Airborne in WWII, among other things. The brief ceremony complete, the convoy of big shiny staff cars sped away. My battalion commander seemed to shrug off the incident of the locked dayroom door. We told the first sergeant to forget it. He did but not quickly.

The next day, I was in my Jeep driving down the company street when I noticed a distinguished Japanese gentleman in a long black overcoat coming down the mess hall steps. ("Mess halls" are now referred to as "dining facilities." In those days, every company had its own. It was a command responsibility that developed character!) He was carrying a large paper bag filled with something. I asked my driver, "Who is that?"

"Sir, that's the company doctor. We give him coffee."

I said, "Company doctor? What does he do?"

The answer revealed the secret to a zero VD statistic: "He gives us penicillin shots!"

Members of that company had so much penicillin in their systems that no VD bug in the world could survive in their blood! We terminated the doctor's contract. No doubt his work had prevented some infections, but possibly compromised immune systems. We found a better way.

This brings me back to the business of measuring and comparing. When we review comparative measures of progress, particularly if it is part of any competition, we need to pay attention to reality and context. General Taylor was a very smart man. He must have had bright people on his staff. Why did nobody say, "General, there's something wrong with that VD data! A company can't go a year with zero infections!" Then perhaps a brief investigation would have led to a more comprehensive and realistic attack on the VD problem.

The real or imagined pressure to submit dishonest reports is a major source of junior leader disenchantment. Only senior officers' professional behavior comes close to forming perceptions about the state of professionalism. Examining statistical competition is worthwhile.

Originality is the most vital of military virtues. B. H. Liddell Hart, 1944.

Thinking about Organizational Energy

Here is one way of visualizing how we might explore and best use the finite energy of the organization—the total human capacity. It is one more conceptual tool for examining and adjusting the organizational climate.

Commanders might profit by visualizing a difference between what we could call *fixed* (or formal process-related) energy and *free* (or informal, spontaneous) energy. The total available effort of all individuals in an organization is finite. People can perform Herculean tasks, of course; we continue to see this in battle heroics. But there is still only so much total energy to be spent. The question is how best to achieve its full potential. The goal is to adjust optimally the ratio of energy-consuming activities between fixed (open the store, keep the trucks moving) and free (plan ahead, experiment).

Fixed and Free Energy in an Organization

Fixed energy is available for:

- standard procedures
- scheduled meetings and required orientations
- routine inspections
- reports and records
- operations orders and after-action reports
- mandatory training

- equipment maintenance
- hauling trash to the landfill
- family maintenance

Free energy, on the other hand, is available for:

- brainstorming
- celebrations
- pickup games
- spare time
- experimenting and innovating
- wandering around
- ad hoc committees

In a "good" organization, fixed energy might be 60 or 70 percent of the total. It takes a heavy percentage to open the shop for business, do the required day-to-day stuff, and comply with all mandated requirements. Fixed energy will always search out and try to capture free energy. If fixed wins, there is not much energy left for planning, experimenting, adjusting, innovating, reflecting, and celebrating. At that point, a system can become clogged, rigid, unimaginative, ponderous, disappointing, and dull.

The first step is to digest the concept. Could categorizing and managing energy help slow down the train and bring more coherence to daily life? A start would be to discuss how energy is being spent and how it might be measured. (Time consumed may be the only viable metric.) Typically, is there any room left for imagining the future, thinking, chewing the fat, less hectic after-action reviews, and some scheduled unscheduled time? It is more than putting free time or "sergeants' time" or recovery time on the training schedule. It is sensitivity to the need to expend energy in line with priorities. It is tougher to do in garrison than in the field. Published training management guidelines may help getting organized for the task.

An appropriate next step is to decide what is sucking up disproportionate energy. Is it meetings, inspections, e-mail responses, reply-by-endorsement to some inquisitive higher headquarters, visitors who just want to say they have visited the front, preparation for no-notice but predictable inspections, daily staff briefings, perfect PowerPoint presentations, mandatory social training, or something else? Just listing the major energy-eaters would be a start. Then their placement in the fixed or free categories may be worth the effort if it leads to a productive discussion of possible adjustments between categories, understanding that there is decreasing wiggle room in schedules the farther down the chain we go. Naturally the view of which activities are productive and which are at best benign vary with organizational levels.

Here is another short form that might be worth its effort by introducing an informed discussion between different echelons. Perhaps the brigade-level commander as one participant and the company commanders as the other. Or the post commander as one and the major subordinate commanders as the other. Would the exercise be worth the time spent? (Similar to the Training Distractor exercise in Note 29 and the APDO instrument in Note 21.)

Chart 9 The Energy Eater Exercise

Comparative Perceptions of Top Three Energy Eaters That Deserve Review	
My top three	**Subordinate top three**
1. *Quarterly budget execution report*	1. *Too many meetings*
2. *Gate checks that slow traffic*	2. *Pre-briefs and perfect PowerPoints*
3. *In and out-processing paperwork*	3. *Processing medical discharges*

Even the bravest cannot fight beyond his strength. Homer, 1000 BC

Note 34

Managing Time to Conserve Energy

We all recognize that managing and protecting time is easier said than done. Both self-discipline and organizational savvy are required to inject efficiency into the schedule and align time with work priorities. Some micromanagement may be needed to enforce time-management policies. When micromanagement is recognized and designed to serve a temporary larger purpose, it can be justified. (For example, policies for soldiers on night duty to sleep undisturbed during daylight hours have a very short half-life unless enforced with near-draconian fervor.)

The first step is to decide whether or not time-management—for self or others—is worth the time. The penchant to continue with the current routine, the emotional energy attending any change, and the inhibiting "If it ain't broke, don't fix it" rationale all offer appetizing excuses for bypassing the issue. The reality is that most of us often waste both the time of self and, more importantly, of numbers of others.

The boss's interest will probably activate numerous ideas about wasted time just hoping for a chance to be heard, even with the whole time-management idea being suspect in many venues. If the time-management notion seems worth a try, the next step is to take a look at "energy eaters" (as in Chart 9) within the context of organizational priorities and prevailing leadership styles.

By their nature, some goals require big chunks of time. A recent example of a legitimate goal eating up disproportionate chunks of a division commanders' day was the battlefield rotation schedule. That noble effort had the commanding general flying or riding for hours most days to visit the troops. Visits to the front are essential; they give the CG a feel for reality, offer an opportunity to listen and evaluate morale and progress, check on understanding of orders, and let the troops know somebody cares. But these stimulating excursions can consume such time and energy that there is little left for other obligations such as visiting with staff.

Once priorities have been outlined—another group exercise-- and their appropriate time expenditures estimated, rough out personal targets like the following:

- personal and emotional fitness: one hour a day
- meetings and visits with commanders: two hours a day
- working with staff on plans, and current crises: two hours a day
- attending meetings decided by others: two hours a day—hopefully less
- tending to relations with higher and adjacent organizations: one hour a day
- thinking time in HQ and wandering around: two hours a day
- routine paperwork: one hour a day

Since there is no such thing as an average day, and many days have only twenty-four hours, such crude, unsophisticated numbers are just that, but perhaps enough to stimulate reflection. The planning process can generate sensitivity to the matter.

Keep track of time expenditures and see how far off reality is from intended. How time is actually spent comes as a shock to most of us. Decide what causes any meaningful difference between assumptions and reality, and brainstorm what might be done, and by whom or what office, to move reality closer to the optimum.

Devise policies to respect and protect the time of subordinate elements. Explain and implement methods for lessening unnecessary intrusions into their daily schedules. Since the details of such policies would vary greatly depending on the environment, here are five specific examples of policies to conserve energy in a garrison setting:

- No calls or e-mails from this headquarters to any subordinate headquarters prior to 1000 hours unless there is a true emergency—a building is on fire, a meeting scheduled for morning hours has been cancelled, or a really hot item of an individual nature has just come in, like Captain Jones has just been selected for a Fulbright scholarship or for flight school or has been picked up DUI. (This protected interlude lets subordinate headquarters get on with their work without attention-diverting calls that could have been made yesterday or can wait for the afternoon.)

- No imposition of any tasking of subordinate headquarters after 1600 hours unless there is a true emergency. (Say the G-3 operations folks at 1700 hours want to add six more trucks to the convoy that departs at 0600 tomorrow. More than likely, this was caused by poor planning. Unless there is a tactical emergency or a commanding general permission for an exception to the rule, the G-3 will have to work with what is at hand. That restriction on the headquarters staff is micromanagement with a reason.)

- No changes to the published training/weekly schedule with less than seven days' notice unless approved by an O-6 or higher leader. (Interestingly, we found that half of the sudden changes that raised hell with coherent family life in garrison, precluded keeping dental appointments, and prompted frantic calls to the ammunition point for an emergency issue were initiated at company and battalion levels.)

- No business e-mails or texts or Tweets or such after the end of the work day, regardless of the brilliance of that midnight idea that can wait until tomorrow.

- If you make an appointment, be on time, thereby respecting the time of others.

Note
35

Meetings and Wasted Time

Meetings are essential. They facilitate coordination, amplify or clarify policy, and process information for decision-making. They also consume an enormous amount of the energy of organizational leaders and staff. Complaints about meetings being a formidable energy drain is widespread, but like the weather nothing is done about it. Unlike the weather, something can be done about it. Uncontrolled meetings are evidence of managerial neglect, a strategic issue worthy of a strategic approach.

Meetings have a formidable capacity to subvert responsibilities for making decisions. They can also perpetuate ambiguity, engender frustration, and subvert initiative all in one fell swoop. They can be a kind of organizational comfort food, satisfying a need for action.

In many organizations, military and otherwise, meetings are uncontrolled. There are few if any rules regarding their number, frequency, duration, intended purpose, or authority to initiate. Some senior officers in the Pentagon probably have fewer than three hours of their working day not attending, preparing for, or reporting the results of meetings. It is unlikely their talents are being efficiently employed. Many are frustrated by inadequate time to create, listen, explore, think, inform, or lead.

Responsibilities of Meeting Attendees

There are two valid reasons for calling a meeting: to share information or to make a decision. Any other reason is suspect. Meetings come in two basic types. One type has a boss in attendance—let's call them B meetings. The other is a meeting of peers with some kind of meeting leader or facilitator, and we'll call them P meetings. In a type B meeting, the boss has the following responsibilities:

- Give all possible advance notice of when, why, and where.
- Show up on time prepared to lead, listen, and, if necessary, make decisions.
- Explain the purpose of the meeting. Is it an orders meeting, where the commander is providing the intent and plan of action, or is it an opportunity to discuss options and explore possibilities?
- Consider the logistics of those attending from remote locations, particularly if in a hostile environment.
- Designate who is responsible for implementing any decisions made at the meeting.
- Invite questions to clarify or confirm decisions. Do this even when there is a tactical emergency ongoing—or perhaps especially when there is a tactical emergency ongoing.
- Keep the meeting on track and adhere to the announced end time. If there must be an extension, take a short break to let participants inform their units.
- Explain plans for any follow-up meetings.
- Participate in a brief evaluation of the meeting. See Chart 10.

In a type P meeting, the participants have the following responsibilities:

- Show up on time, having done their homework.
- Listen completely before commenting.
- Be direct and candid with comments.
- Help with finding solutions and drafting conclusions.
- Use electronic devices with respect for others.
- Take notes so they can report results of the meeting.
- Ask questions about any item that is unclear, and persist until they receive a coherent answer or an order to cease and desist.

- Participate in a brief evaluation of the meeting.
- Share meeting notes with others. Spread the good news and insights.

General Guidelines for Meetings

There should be a policy declaring who has authority to call a meeting for which agencies/sections, and with what required advance notice. (In tactical emergencies, there are exceptions. But not every day can be an emergency, even in combat.) The executive officer or staff director should compile, produce, and distribute periodically a review of staff meetings of all types at all levels: numbers and agencies involved, time consumed, decisions reached, and opinions on future need for the meeting.

Meetings must have set times to start and finish and a requirement that all meetings have at least a brief record completed before adjournment—perhaps one page or a couple PowerPoints—indicating agreed-upon conclusions and recommendations. If there are no conclusions or recommendations, why did we meet?

Periodic meetings can generate a life of their own, can continue forever without justification, and warrant a sunset clause that prompts a periodic review of their essentiality. Because global teleconferencing can intrude twenty-four hours a day, the purpose, length, frequency, and participation of these conferences should be evaluated with stringent criteria. Somebody needs to be in charge of the net, and somebody else needs to be keeping score.

Every meeting scheduled to last an hour or more should reserve the final ten minutes for a cleanup and evaluate session. All meetings should be evaluated at the site of the accident by the participants, with results going to the senior host and others culpable. The form shown in Chart 10 takes about ninety seconds to complete. Warn/threaten participants of its use in advance.

Chart 10 Meeting Assessment Form

Meeting hosted by: _____ Date: _____

1. Planned start time: _____ Actual start time: _____

2. Planned end time: _____ Actual end time: _____

3. Meeting purpose: 5 (very clear) to 1 (ambiguous) _____

4. Conduct of meeting: 5 (efficient) to 1 (disorganized) _____

5. Meeting conclusions: 5 (specific, useful) to 1 (none reached) _____

6. Worth doing again: 5 (yes, necessary) to 1 (absolutely not) _____

7. Other comments: _____

Note 36

Staff Leadership

Ever since King Gustavus Adolphus published guidelines for staff organization and behavior in the seventeenth century, the subject has been food for discussion. In musings about staff operations, an image of staff officers as nervous bureaucrats is often contrasted with the heroic image of their colleagues serving in line units. It is a dysfunctional cultural stereotype in an era greatly dependent on staff productivity. It is particularly inappropriate since most officers will serve many more days on a staff than in the chain of command in line organizations.

For decades, studies have found morale to be significantly lower in staff than in line organizations. Some of this difference is the consequence of a culture that prides itself on being commander-oriented. But problems with staff morale arise from deeper, less philosophical beginnings. It is in essence a leadership issue, not simply an artifact of a warrior culture.

Dissatisfaction with aspects of Pentagon staff service has been revealed in a variety of reports. A notable 1973 article by Colonel Mike Malone, "The Prize," described an incoherent, demoralizing staff environment.[54] That article led to the author's two-hour lunch with the Army Chief of Staff, followed by a brief spasm of interest in the world of the Pentagon staff officer.

Staff morale and productivity are neglected topics in most institutions. Inattention to

---

[54] It is worth digging up this article from the December 1985 issue of *Army* magazine and reading "The Subordinates," a classic on direct leadership.

staff leadership is a self-imposed, culturally facilitated obstacle to high-quality decision-making. The division commanders in the 2004 and 2010 studies generally received solid grades for leadership. They proudly mentioned their battlefield circulation schedules and frequent interaction with subordinates in the field. None mentioned how they had toured the buildings or vans or tents where their staffs were laboring, encouraging questions and clarifying any recent policy directives. Neither the division commanders, the members of the staff, nor the subordinate commanders were satisfied with staff productivity during operations in Iraq and Afghanistan. Parts of the divisions being assembled shortly prior to deployment with no time to get to know staff personalities may have contributed to the problem.

The institutional roles and responsibilities of staff officers are well defined. For example, the *Army Commander and Staff Officer Guide,* published in September 2011,[55] is a remarkably comprehensive and useful handbook. It covers in detail every aspect and expectation for performance, including a section on the need and method to assess accomplishment. Lucid conceptual guidance from doctrine and military school curricula has not resolved a recurring discontent. Creative leadership can work wonders in a staff as well as in a unit.

> No military force in war can accomplish anything worthwhile unless there is in back of it the work of an efficient, loyal, and dedicated staff. Lieutenant General Hunter Liggett[56]

---

[55] HQDA, ATTP 5-0.1. This 2011 publication provides comprehensive and detailed coverage of staff work. Any existing staff problems are not from an absence of coherent doctrinal guidance.

[56] Lieutenant General Hunter Liggett, 1857–1935, was a thoughtful, respected leader who participated in campaigns from the Indian Wars through World War I.

Guidance in the 1951 edition of *The Officers Guide* indicates we have been working on staff matters regularly over the years.

> "The staff serves the troops as well as the commander. Good staff work requires the staff to know and appreciate fully the situation of the troops, their morale, their state of training … and all other conditions affecting their efficiency. This information can be obtained by intimate contact and observation, but it cannot be secured by remaining behind a desk."[57]

Other ageless wisdom was also included in that book that was a kind of bible then.

The problem seems not commonly related to a paucity of staff resources, although personnel turbulence common at lower levels can be a factor. Low staff morale most often results from lack of attention to the climate in which the staff functions.

Recent Studies and Recurring Phenomenon

Surveys of Army headquarters in the Pentagon conducted at the request of the Chief of Staff in 2011 and 2012 highlighted not-uncommon problems. The plus was that a busy staff stood still to be studied, the participants thoughtful, candid, and appreciative. A frequent complaint was that everybody up the chain can say no, but few can or are willing to say yes. The "or are willing" was not inconsequential. Another complaint saw staff processes as cumbersome, often untrusting, and routinely encumbered with unnecessary layers of concurrence. Perhaps more importantly, none of the couple hundred staff officers who participated in the surveys recalled any earlier investigation of staff working environment or institutional interest in the sources of their frustration. (Any

---

[57] *The Officers Guide*, 368. It makes more sense now than when I quickly skipped over it in 1952. A hard book to locate, but a real gem that reveals changes in protocol but consistency over time in professional values.

issues regarding the role of a professional civilian staff working for appointed executives in conjunction with uniformed staff operations were not explored in that survey.)

In response to perceived inability for the large, traditional, often inflexible staff structure to provide timely response, many general officers created small ad hoc cells. These mini-staffs comprised of bright and energetic officers recruited by the generals did provide some quick responses. Ultimately, it was at a steep price. These ad hoc special staff groups absorbed top talent, complicated already complex procedures for concurrence and decisions, and lacked the resources to research issues or coordinate actions, often pressing the traditional staff section for short-fuse assistance.

These following three items from the 2011 and 2012 Pentagon surveys received the most problematic ratings from the participating staff officers. They represent more leadership-related than resource-related phenomenon:

- "We do not have problems with conflicting guidance from different sources."
- "Our meetings normally are efficient, on time, and with useful conclusions and coherent records."
- "Deadlines for taskings are typically reasonable and based on legitimate needs of staff leaders."

There was some good, albeit somewhat perplexing, news. Most leaders on the staff were seen by subordinates as good leaders who were entangled in a staff bureaucracy and protocol they could not reconstruct. The quality of the people assigned to the staff— excepting a few individuals obviously mal-assigned outside their area of expertise—was not a concern. Real or imagined interference in the staffing processes by influential outside agencies was in some areas a source of discontent. Resolving that delicate human dynamic is primarily a leadership task at very high levels, as between senior civilian and military leaders.

A few—or many—good leaders on a staff focusing on re-engineering their own domain will not significantly change the prevailing climate, just as a set of good company commanders cannot restore totally an unhealthy battalion climate. Incremental change from the bottom up in a conservative, busy organization has little chance for sustained impact. There has to be a comprehensive, synchronized overhaul led from upstairs. Any renovation in staff process, structure, or resources needs to be embedded firmly to preclude unnecessary future repetition of the exercise.

Staff senior leaders must model the critical behaviors needed to facilitate climate change. Undoubtedly the most consequential is the ability to tolerate criticism of procedures and listen to suggestions for change.

The two items below from that staff survey were interestingly very positive, even as frustration with the overall climate continued. They confirm that the basic issue is structural and cultural, and not primarily a deficiency of good leadership among staff officers. The lack of institutional progress in designing a staff and formulating processes that can keep up with the twenty-first-century environment is a failure at the strategic leader level.

- "You can tell it like it is to the boss; we don't hide bad news."
- "I am encouraged to ask for clarification if mission guidance is incomplete or ambiguous."

The Staff Tune-Up Process

The solution starts with recognition of the issue: staff leadership and productivity need attention. Then we can use a broad approach similar to that in the "Master Plan for Organizational Leadership" at Note 31. Recognizing that military staffs range in size from a couple dozen mostly junior folks at battalion level to several hundred experienced people led by flag officers (the Joint Staff is now limited by law to 1,627 individuals), the specifics of each step obviously differ in their application. A staff working under a broad charter can be a source for innovative ideas that cut across unit or branch boundaries, but creativity is often bottled up by protocol or structure.

The concepts for staff renewal apply universally.

Step 1: Develop a common understanding of the staff mission and priorities. ("Mission" may take some time for a useful definition. "Priorities" will take longer.) In particular, answer the following:

- What are the expectations for communicating with and serving higher, lower, and adjacent/partner organizations? What are the priorities?
- What are the guidelines regarding staff responsibility for monitoring and assisting operating units in executing command directives?

Step 2: Design a procedure that will ensure understanding by all parties—commanders and involved staffs—of the commander's intent in orders. Explain and reiterate this process often, and encourage feedback on its effectiveness in obliterating ambiguity. In particular, answer the following:

- How does the commander ensure that his intent is clear to those who will execute?
- What routine actions can subordinates take to clarify orders and confirm priorities?
- What guidelines ensure that any "clarification" of the order by deputies or staff officers remains consistent with the commander's intent?

Step 3: Define the authority for approval of staff papers, staff policies, and staff tasks; for amendment or redefinition of staff directives or procedures; and for engagement with other staffs or agencies as either an individual or staff spokesman. This is an opportunity to use the true-or-false policy quiz format in Note 25. It is also a chance to explore how decisions get modified at various levels, intentionally or otherwise, as they pass downward and sideways through various paths and gates to the intended recipients

Step 4: Remind all concerned of three basic rules:

1. We speak truth to power on this staff.
2. We never fudge the data.
3. We work to help our subordinate units just as we work to help our boss.

Subordinate staff officers have a particular obligation to confront the boss when offhand comments, inadequate guidance, or inadequate coordination create even mild incoherence. Reluctance of subordinates to confront potentially unethical practice has contributed to colossal disasters. This heavy obligation to uphold standards requires continuing reinforcement by the institution. The immediate boss has an obligation to maintain an open climate and to set the example for telling truth to power.

Step 5: Take the pulse of the staff by using a suitable staff climate survey instrument. Pertinent statements include the following:

Chart 11 Staff Survey Sample Items

Sample Staff Survey Items	Evaluation
1. In my section, our goals and priorities are clear.	
2. We can take reasonable risks; no "zero defects" mentality here.	
3. My tour on this staff will contribute to my professional development.	
4. We focus on substantive matters, not on "show and tell" projects.	

An example of a climate survey tailored for staffs is in Appendix A.

Step 6: Assess staff performance by gathering the views of adjacent and lower units on its effectiveness. After they recover from the shock of being asked for their views, there needs to be an understanding regarding confidentiality of resulting data. Here are eight questions for such an approach. It is kind of a "staff 270" compared to an "individual 360"—the boss need not participate. These eight items in Chart 12 are enough to get a useful sense of effectiveness but brief enough to encourage participation. Results of the survey should be discussed with the commanders whose staffs participated, obviously having approved their staff's participation in the first place.

Chart 12 Staff Performance Feedback Form

Staff Performance Feedback Form (SPFF)	Evaluation
1. We have a convenient point of contact for communication with that staff.	
2. We have an honest, candid exchange of information with that staff.	
3. That staff understands our needs.	
4. That staff tailors its products and considers our deadlines.	
5. That staff responds to requests in a timely manner.	
6. That staff is open to suggestions about its operation.	
7. That staff provides suggestions for improving our operation.	
8. Morale on that staff looks pretty good from our viewpoint.	

Step 7: Convene a team to make sense of the data generated by the prior six steps and create a plan and goals for staff development. Expose the plan widely for comment. Refine and advertise specific goals.

Step 8: Create a plan for assessing progress toward whatever goals are set in Step 7.

Step 9: Repeat Steps 4 and 5 periodically. Remember that institutional memory is short and that the folks who participated in the exercise and gave feedback last year might have disappeared.

> A yes man on the staff is a menace to the commander. One with courage to express his convictions is an asset. Major General Orlando Ward,[58] 1934

---

[58] Major General Orlando Ward, 1891–1972, fought in Mexico, World War I, and World War II. His relief as commander of the 1AD in Europe remains controversial, with assertions that political expedience was the primary cause.

Notes from the Notes of Part 6

PART 7

Following, Learning, Teaching, and Serving

Everybody thinks of changing humanity
and nobody thinks of changing himself.

Leo Tolstoy

Followership

Except for God and maybe the chairman of the Federal Reserve, all leaders in organizations are also followers. Even more interesting, many of our followers are also leaders. In both roles, some obligations are hard and fast: protect public property, follow orders, wear only authorized decorations, etc. Some obligations are born of the profession: learn essential skills, place mission before self, have courage. Others come from fundamental values that anchor civilized behavior: play fair, protect the weak, treat others as you would like to be treated.

As loyal followers, we have particular obligations and opportunities. In meeting those obligations and handling those opportunities, a fundamental assumption is that both leader and follower want the organization to succeed.

For this discussion, *follower* and *subordinate* are basically interchangeable. Technically, *follower* might more closely describe a voluntary commitment to a cause or a person without legal subordination. But *followership* is meaningful in describing the role of loyal subordinates. Whatever we name it, it carries a professional obligation to behave with the same attention to values of competence, commitment, candor, and courage that we expect of leaders.

Here are some rules for followers. Clearly, their applicability depends on the nature of the leader–follower organizational relationship. The platoon leader who sees the company commander daily has different opportunities to respond and assist than the brigade commander who might interact with the division commander a few times a month, or the division commander who may be distant from the corps commander. Loyal, disciplined following from afar is a precious institutional commodity. In every circumstance, the follower is obliged to do the following:

- **Prepare for the particular job.** As time permits, refresh on tactics and techniques peculiar to the situation. There is information someplace about the current mission, resources, and reputation. There will be information also on the reputation of your new boss, but don't spend much time on that. Understanding a leader's style is helpful, but the main point is to work based on professional principles, not on individual idiosyncrasies.

- **Take the pulse of the situation.** Find out how best to help the boss and the organization by checking the state of the climate, the quality of relationships, the clarity of mission, the adequacy of resources. Read basic references on current plans, operations, standard operating procedures, and any notes from predecessors. (Having done this, you may find you are one of the better-informed members of the community!)

- **Work to clarify orders for yourself and others.** If there is the least bit of ambiguity about your assigned mission—not about how it is to be carried out but the mission and priorities itself—do everybody a favor by pushing the boss until there is no need for subsequent meetings to decide what the boss really wants. If he is busy and irritable, do it anyway. You only live once. Developing clarity of intent is the biggest gift you can give your boss, the staff, and your subordinates.

> Great leaders and followers are always engaged in a creative collaboration.
> Warren Bennis

- **Ask the boss about expectations for your role.** This is more important at higher levels, where expectations can be vague. Even at the small-unit level, spend as much time as the situation allows getting clear on how the boss expects you to function. Is there some particular division of work, or boundaries on your authority, or particularly sensitive relationships that will be important? (If the boss says, "If I didn't think you knew how to do the job, I wouldn't have hired you!" you might try again later after he has figured out an answer.)

- **Carry out orders as though they were yours.** Give the execution of the order every possible support, using initiative to make it better within the bounds of the boss's intent. (We assume the orders are legal and ethical.)

- **Be optimistic and generate energy.** Enthusiasm is contagious in every direction. It is almost as potent an energizer as humor.

- **Be a responsible, non-public critic.** If you have concerns about the practicality of an order—and the enemy is not coming in over the wire at the moment—make them known. If your concerns are considered and rejected, move out and do your best without complaint. If your concerns involve ethics or legality, that is a different matter. Persist in exploring the issue. Loyalty to the boss is fundamental, but some loyalties supersede others.

- **Help the boss with decision-making.** Help with advice on the substance of the decision, methods of decision-making, and review of progress. Is he reaching out to all available experts? Is he over-dependent on a single source? Do you know of a prior study that might be useful? Does he have a habit of punishing the messenger who brings a different perspective?

- **If a clear opportunity presents itself, provide respectful, candid behavioral feedback.** This is delicate stuff. A suitable opportunity may never arise if the boss has difficulty appreciating subordinate input. However, a trusted follower might be able to make a unique contribution. Reminding about clarifying guidance and listening to ideas may be tolerable.

- **Find ways to save the boss's time and energy.** Thoughtful followers are creative in examining how their boss uses time, exploits technology, and gathers and analyzes data. Particularly in higher headquarters, a review of schedules may reveal too many meetings, too many video conferences, and not enough—or too much—wandering around. At some point, it might be acceptable to suggest the boss go home early once in a while, not be at the line of departure tomorrow, and stifle outgoing communications at the end of the day.

- **Keep any disagreements private.** Closed-door discussions should stay closed. Loyal followers do not gossip.

- **Ask the boss once in a while—preferably not during a ground assault or a contentious conference—how you could better support him or her.** In a more perfect world, the boss would automatically provide performance feedback. But that is rare, particularly at senior levels.

- **Give advice based on your convictions, not on what might please the boss.** Define the boundary between authentic support and self-serving ingratiation. Loyal followers tell it like it is and deal with the consequences.

- **Make a pledge to yourself that you will take action if you see your boss moving into illegal or unethical activities.** Be assured there are professional values that overwhelm loyalty to the current boss. If you have the essential facts, do not avoid acting because you "don't have access to all relevant information." The first, tough step in taking action is to confront the boss. Even that norm could be bypassed if his behavior is outside the bounds of professional conduct. This is a loyal follower's obligation to the institution.

"You know, Foley, I have only one eye; I have a right to be blind sometimes— I really do not see the signal." Nelson to his flag captain, having had his attention invited to Sir Hyde Parker's signal to discontinue engagement, 1801.

Once Upon a Time, Long, Long Ago …

… we had an interesting battalion commander—a decorated WWII veteran—whose mood swings were considerable. Bizarre adventures in our organization were not uncommon. He was not a toxic leader, but he was incompetent and dangerous. He would qualify as destructive.

We company commanders did what any loyal group of followers would do after repeatedly being refused an audience to argue for a change of orders: we banded together to protect our soldiers, the government's property, and our Army's reputation. Our battalion reported directly to a division headquarters that was geographically hours away by road and philosophically from a different planet.

This particular mission first came from the operations officer, as I recall. "The colonel is concerned about maintenance. He wants to have a tank race to see which company has the best maintenance. His tank will represent Headquarters Company."

Our collective first reaction was disbelief. Not total disbelief, because a few weeks earlier at the end of a commanders meeting, we were admonished for not having ordered antifreeze, since winter was fast approaching. It was a stern warning, and we were dismissed without an opportunity to raise questions. We were puzzled because our M-46 tanks had air-cooled engines. But that was finally resolved without major embarrassment, since each company had one tank-recovery vehicle based on the aging M-4 chassis that did have a water-cooled engine. But I digress.

Early on, we went to any battalion staff officer who would listen. However, the colonel had announced that he would tolerate no discussion on the topic. Furthermore, he noted that our objections probably came from fear of revealing how slow and improperly maintained our tanks were compared to his. The gap between us first lieutenant company commanders and that lieutenant colonel battalion commander was wide, wide. (As we move on to higher ranks, it is easy to forget how big the gap can be between company commanders with three or four years' service and their seasoned battalion commanders.)

Now this exercise, apart from the fact that the relationship between tank speed and maintenance status is near zero, had potentially serious consequences. Our M-46 tanks were about forty tons, and at about 3,000 RPM could move just above thirty miles per hour on the flat. The designated area for the race was a dirt track oval about a half mile long just outside the post, probably used for some kind of auto racing years before. The vaguely defined grass lanes were about ten yards wide. There was a small raised wooden viewing platform that could hold maybe ten or twelve people on the long side of the oval.

On the designated day, there were five tanks present near the starting line: one from each of the four tank companies, plus the battalion commander's tank. We had done a lot of intercompany coordination to see if we could get through the morning without getting anybody killed. I can't remember how the starting positions were decided, but I think there were two tanks in the first row and three in the second—all with engines running, waiting for the flag to drop. The colonel and his staff, some very worried maintenance officers, and all of us company commanders were huddled on the platform thinking about how the headlines might read if our plan went astray.

Our plan was to make it as much of a race as we could while not endangering anybody—including anybody on the flimsy reviewing stand. Each of our drivers knew exactly how things were to go. Each, that is, except for the battalion commander's driver, who had not been invited to our clandestine planning sessions.

The race was now on. Picture five 40-ton tanks taking three trips around a tiny half-mile course and having to make it look like a contest. We were holding our breath and wondering why this was happening and if we should just have had a mutiny and been done with it. After two laps with no accidents and a speed high enough to look like a race, there came from the colonel's tank a high screeching noise. Then it leapt ahead of the other contenders.

Obviously, the colonel's mechanic had disabled the engine-speed governor that was on all those M-46 tanks. That engine must have been red hot on all cylinders. It left our machines in the dust. It was wonderful to watch. The battalion commander had emerged victorious, and nobody got hurt.

The colonel said, "I told you so. Get with your maintenance programs!"

We all saluted and said, "Yes sir."

It was a Saturday. We took the rest of the day off. I think we had a few beers. I can't recall any further discussions with the colonel about tank maintenance.

Good subordinates might collude if necessary—within limits—to help the boss and protect the troops. This adventure tested the limit of responsible protecting. We all should have gone to jail had anybody been hurt. But in the context of the moment, as a separate battalion many miles from anybody else, and considering the colonel's good points as well as not-so-good points, it made sense then. Sounds really weird sixty years later.

If you have a yes-man working for you, one of you is redundant. General Colin Powell

Continuing to Learn and Grow as Leaders

Having then been steeped in the doctrine, traditions, and practice of leadership in the military for more than three decades, my move to employment at the Center for Creative Leadership (CCL) might be seen as entering a different universe. But it was not. Familiar ideals about service and integrity and excellence prevailed similarly in both outfits. During nine challenging and rewarding years at CCL, the following are some lessons learned—or relearned:

- Civilians are different, but few are fatally flawed.
- There are no leadership or management secrets in the business world we in the military haven't heard. Applying the concepts is the key.
- The default setting of all known hierarchies is "stupid."
- There is a big difference between knowing and doing.
- Genetics and childhood experiences influence our adult leadership style.
- Many leadership studies have a problem: leaders being studied as successful might not have been good leaders after all. Criteria for success remain squishy.
- Nobody knows how to pick only the right people for promotion.
- Self-awareness is serious business and gets more serious as life moves on.
- Successful senior executives need to keep learning, as counterintuitive as that might be for strong personalities in their mature years.
- Civilians are also patriotic and passionate about their work, but they don't make night moves.

The Need for Continuing Education

The need for organized education for senior leaders in our Army was recognized long ago. It may not have been as apparent then to most senior leaders as it was to Secretary of War Elihu Root. He set up the Army War College in 1901, followed soon after by the General Staff and Service College at Fort Leavenworth. The birth of these notable institutions was perhaps the most significant outcome of the poorly managed Spanish American War.

What is new for the officer corps today and for the executive cadre in most leading organizations is the added emphasis on post-Leavenworth, post–War College, post-graduate education. There is increasing realization that much knowledge has a short half-life and that leader competence and behavior remain the major contributors to productivity. One of the particular demands of the twenty-first-century environment is relentless competition for the kind of leader talent needed to lead bright young Americans and motivate them to spend a meaningful part of their lives in noble institutions.

Even with contributions from in-house military colleges, opportunities for a sabbatical with industry, weeks at joint schools, and semesters at noted think tanks, the fact persists that leader development is mostly a self-help operation. If we become spectacularly successful, it is increasingly counterintuitive to listen and learn; we are busy, we have heard that all before, and "I must have done it right to get promoted."

How We Continue to Learn

We learn in three domains. The first is *trainable functions* and includes skills like firing a weapon, flying a helicopter, reading a map, or delivering a briefing. (Some obviously require more mental acuity than others.)

Second, we have an array of *conceptual or cognitive competencies* that can be nourished to some extent by various types of education and feedback. We expose students to ideas of critical thinking, strategic planning, cultural diversity, intergovernmental operations, and such.

The third domain is both the most difficult and the primary source of differentiation between success and failure, particularly at senior levels. That domain concerns *behavior*: adjusting self-performance to the demands of context and to institutional and subordinate expectations. Biographies of leaders are unique sources of insight in this area. Make a lot of notes in their margins. (Examples are in Appendix C.)

Adrian Wolfberg at the Army War College published an excellent 2016 article on how three- and four-star generals continued their on-the-job learning.[59] The specific subject was handling the complex collection and interpretation of intelligence in Iraq and Afghanistan. The observation at hand was the introspective manner in which these senior officers continued their efforts to learn and apply new paradigms.

Once again, few senior leaders fail because of lack of technical knowledge; not many fail because of lack of understanding of global politics (that is "not many," not "none"). Some are hampered by their lack of insight about organizational dynamics— the systems by which we communicate intent and monitor progress. But most parts of systems leadership can be taught. Again, most who derail are victims of interpersonal deficiencies: not listening, not keeping promises, not gaining the trust of subordinates or peers, and not seeing the big picture.

The Self-Awareness Challenge

As mentioned, most deficiencies in continuing to learn among generally healthy, functioning adults stem from lack of awareness about their true skills and the impact of their behavior on others. We might place the leader population in three categories:

1. "I have little interest in how my behavior affects others. That is their problem, not mine."

---

[59] Wolfberg, "When Generals Consume Intelligence." There was apparent intent in their deliberations to be open and address problems individually and collectively from a variety of perspectives. Whether culturally-induced or a result of the selection process, it seemed an affirmation of capability to learn from self and others.

2. "I have an interest in how my behavior affects others, and I am willing to take a look and work on it if necessary."

3. "I am consumed by introspection and anxious about the impression I make."

Even for individuals open to learning about themselves, it is often difficult to receive useful feedback. It is possible that any lack of interest in the subject is an indicator of minimal intellectual curiosity, a clear limit to effectiveness at senior levels of command. It is also possible that structured interest in self remains for some an uncomfortable if not distasteful endeavor. There is little doubt that leaders whose view of themselves is notably more positive than the assessments held by their subordinates are likely to be marginally effective as leaders.[60]

Since leader development, particularly at mid and senior levels, rests considerably on self-development there is a related powerful premise: "I am interested in my continuing development as a leader." Self-coaching can begin by simply recording observations about leader behavior, noting the distinguishing features and responses to effective and ineffective behavior, and visualizing how such behaviors can be adopted or avoided.

It is difficult to improve and to confirm progress in the awareness domain absent some kind of baseline from which to measure progress. The best way of getting a useful, reliable look at our strengths and weaknesses, and constructing such a baseline, is through the 360-degree assessment process with self, boss, peers, and subordinates contributing. That assumes the 360 instrument is valid and that subordinates and peers feel safe giving candid responses.

The characteristics mentioned earlier as enabling effective leader behavior were cognitive power, need to be engaged, capacity for clarity of expression, energy level, empathy, and emotional resilience. Among those, clarity of expression and possibly empathy might be the most suitable targets for improvement. Clarity would be easiest to improve, assuming the necessary cognitive power and determination were at hand.

---

[60] Yammarino, *Understanding Self-Perception Accuracy*. This manuscript describes relationships between awareness and effectiveness, among other useful observations.

Enhancing empathy would probably require a more sophisticated and lengthy regimen—but if the will is there, notable results are possible.

Bypassing characteristics and attending to discrete, productive behaviors, would be the most efficient use of competent feedback. The twenty-nine items in the survey designed for the division commander studies earlier mentioned in Note 12 and contained in Appendix A would be suitable for use in the 360 process. Competence in behaviors—such as "Clearly explains missions," "Does not play favorites," "Welcomes new ideas"—are important in any situation and amenable to improvement if that need is confirmed.

To optimally improve as a leader within an organization, the boss must be an active participant. That includes being aware of the specific goals, knowing some of the details of the program, and arranging to monitor progress. Even simply acknowledging that the subordinate is scheduled for formal schooling or is launching a self-improvement initiative can make a profound difference in the outcome.

Progress can be measured—albeit imprecisely—in three ways. We can make notes for ourselves about what we think we learned (a journal of some kind); we can get feedback on the job from boss, peers, subordinates, inspectors, or assessors; and in some situations, we can measure changes in organizational productivity based on our contribution. All of these measurements are tough to capture in a busy organization. (See Note 32 on Measurement.) Evaluating the results of leader development efforts remains a weak link in the educational and developmental business.

Notes from an Old but Relevant Leadership Study

A study of behaviors of Army leaders was published in July 1971 by the U.S. Army War College titled *Leadership for the 1970s: USAWC Study of Leadership for the Professional Soldier.* This was a neat approach—perhaps groundbreaking. It gathered responses from 1,800 soldiers, from junior noncommissioned officers to general officers. It was later replicated with about 20,000 participants with the same general results. Data were presented from several grade groupings (Junior NCO: E-4-6, Senior NCO: E-7-9,

Junior Company Grade: lieutenants, Senior Company Grade: captains, Junior Field Grade: majors and lieutenant colonels, and Senior Field Grade: colonels) and in different formats.

In the study, respondents described the importance and prevalence of forty-three leader behaviors (not dissimilar to the behaviors described in the 2004 and 2010 division commander studies previously mentioned) in contributing to leader effectiveness. The study recorded which leader behaviors were seen as deviating in what degree from desired standards and which behaviors had what we named "self-delusion potential" or "perceptual shortfall"—the difference between self-assessment and observer assessment. Capturing that data by grade levels appears unique.

Here are the behaviors with the most difference between what colonels thought they were doing and what their subordinates saw them doing. There is no argument about who the experts were here. These particular revelations about specific aspects of self-awareness in 1971 may or may not have changed much in the intervening five decades. But the salient point is that, if we choose to do so, we can get a fix on this important slice of the institutional leadership pie.

The following Items had the greatest negative difference between colonel's perception and subordinates' perception:

- He stood up for his subordinates even though it made him unpopular with his superior.
- He counseled, trained, and developed his subordinates.
- He constructively criticized poor performance.
- He was willing to support his subordinates even when they made mistakes.
- He criticized subordinates in front of others.

These misperceptions have consequences. It is perceptions here that count. Listening to subordinate opinion provided by some legitimate mode (such as the 360 or in some circumstances a climate survey) seems the logical solution. There are no current data I have seen that indicate these misperceptions are no longer with us.

There were about a hundred general officers in the sample population. At that time, the unspoken word was that publishing details of the collective opinions of their subordinates was just not done. We have since become appropriately more open in that area. General Officer data were not included in the widely distributed reports in 1971 but are available in Army War College files and were captured as well in an unpublished document by one of the study co-leaders.[61] It seems unlikely, based on informal observations from senior Army school and Center for Creative Leadership faculty members, that the typical personality of general officers has changed measurably. That typical personality—with wide differences and clear options for selective improvement—is very healthy.

The 1971 views from subordinates showed them to be "highly pleased" overall with general officer leadership. Subordinates in this study rated the generals higher on leader behaviors than the generals rated themselves—a normally healthy pattern. Here are the top five behaviors in rank order of subordinate view of importance:

1. Being willing to support subordinates.
2. Being aware of morale and attempting to improve it.
3. Communicating effectively with subordinates.
4. Being technically competent to perform their duties.
5. Approaching each task in a positive manner.

These behaviors came from a list of forty-three that covered the same areas included

---

[61] Malone, D. M. "Leadership at General Officer Level," an undated document circa 1975, uses the total 30,000 response data to describe various aspects of general officer leadership. It is in hand and filed at the Army War College under Ref Files Leadership # 2312. It would seem useful to replicate and compare 1971 with 2017. The heart of the matter is not how positively any grades are viewed typically by their subordinates but which particular behaviors are most important in creating impressions regarding leader effectiveness. The self-delusion factor computations seem particularly useful in contributing to continuing development as a leader at any level.

in the 2004 and 2010 Army War College studies of division commanders. Both lists came from a synthesis of Army leadership doctrine and were consistent with prevailing academic literature. Subordinate views of the relative importance of behaviors do not seem to change much over time. Communication, loyalty downward, attending to climate and morale, and attending to decision-making are confirmed repeatedly, and were prominent in the 1971 study.

A Very Brief Recipe for Self-Improvement

The cost-benefit ratio of this effort is extraordinary: When younger, work on speaking. When older, work on listening. Find a candid coach. As speaking and listening skills improve, a cluster of other desirable behaviors will improve also.

Leadership and learning are indispensable to each other. John F. Kennedy

Note 39

Military Leadership in the Twenty-First Century

In the twenty-first, as in all prior centuries, organizational leaders have the dual requirement of addressing the task at hand while nurturing values critical to future institutional health. Those tasks are compounded today by accelerating changes in technology amid a global atmosphere of political, societal, and economic unrest.

Crossbow, saddle, Gatling gun, telegraph, balloon, tank, submarine, aircraft carrier, nuclear power, the silicon chip, and robots all modified war and its preparation. Perhaps the saddest commentary on the "progress" of civilization is that wars continue. Nowhere on a plausible horizon rests a conflict-free world. How best to form and sustain an effective military institution thus remains a cogent issue. America cannot, and should not, avoid a primary role in bringing some form of coherence to a dangerous world. As Spiderman's Uncle Ben and other revered scholars have noted, "With great power comes great responsibility!"

Today's world demands a military institution both efficient and effective. Both derive from innovative use of material and human resources, sustained by values and practices derived from experience. Institutions perpetuate excellence by codifying best practice and adjusting to the environment through education, indoctrination, training, and supervision.

Attributes of a Twenty-First Century Leader

Principles, requisite behaviors, and attributes are based more on unchanging human nature than on contemporary technology or tactics. However, there may be value in considering a list of attributes particularly relevant to the current environment, most of which would have made the list compiled for any era. Again, it is the particular behaviors in implementation of a principle or an attribute that are critical to good leadership.

1. **Passion for mission**—a loyal, enthusiastic, unselfish commitment to the mission and values of the institution

2. **Moral courage**—determination to confront ethical issues head-on and to remain true to the highest standards of integrity regardless of personal considerations

3. **Decision-making agility**—a high level of cognitive capacity combined with an intellectual versatility that discriminates and adjusts to the situation at hand

4. **Emotional and physical resilience**—the capacity to withstand the continuous pressures associated with military activities

5. **Comfort with action**—willingness to make bold decisions, take the initiative, set the example, and lead even when personally or professionally hazardous

6. **Self-awareness**—a reasonably accurate assessment of motives, drives, strengths, and weaknesses, and the likely impact of one's behavior on others

7. **Sensitivity to context**—alertness to the nuances of the environment and to the background from which decisions are made, implemented, and evaluated

8. **Capacity to trust**—the ability and willingness to trust and rely on others

9. **Commitment to learn and renew**—a strong, informed intent to search for new skills and insights, and to remain open to the ideas of others. This includes comfort with advances in technology and an understanding of relevant societal trends.

10. **Communication skills**—the ability to present ideas to a variety of audiences using available tools and techniques

American Society and the Military

With knowledge of military life in general and ground combat operations in particular perhaps at an all-time low among the general population, members of Congress, and many appointed officials in the defense establishment, military leaders must be world-class teachers. The American public, broadly supportive and appreciative of its military, is increasingly distant from its culture.

American society supports its military in four areas:

- It provides the funds to design, buy, operate, and repair installations and machines.
- It provides psychological support, sense of legitimate purpose, and feeling of honorable service and appreciation to its military members.
- It makes available to our armed forces men and women who enter a subculture distinctly different but not detached from the parent society.
- It codifies through Congress and the executive branch rules and regulations under which military members serve.

Our society also has rather clear expectations of its military: be prepared to fight and win, and do so while respecting the rights and dignity of individuals within, served by, and in contact with our military. In order to meet the legitimate expectations of the American people, there must be attention to all aspects of leadership. In this Note we'll look at a few contemporary realities deserving notice.

Today, about three in ten American youth meet the minimum requirements for enlisting in America's Army. It is interesting that while we have a high percentage of youth drifting toward computer-enabled diabetic obesity, the smaller qualifying cohort still produces Medal of Honor recipients—Soldiers, Sailors, Airmen, Marines, and Coast Guardsmen—whose performance today would make heroes of yesterday proud. Emerging from a physically "softening" populace, those serving in the military from 1970s to the early part of this century have voiced few complaints about discipline too strong or standards too high.[62] While there may be formidable evidence that part of our youth is "going to hell in a handbasket," America keeps producing winners.

But given the dwindling percentage of our population who are fit to serve—and the increasing competition for astute and energetic people—can we recruit and retain the adventurous, resilient folks needed to work the tip of the spear and also manage a multibillion-dollar enterprise? Can members of the millennial generation who may feel entitled and skeptical of structure be converted to enthusiastic members of a team? The answer to those questions depends greatly on whether leaders can, by example and organizational outcome, retain the trust of the American people. They must build work environments that satisfy the legitimate expectations of bright, ambitious young people—particularly those who self-select to enter the military profession. For economic and political reasons, for the foreseeable future, the days of a military draft are over. (It is interesting that for the life of the American Army there have been only small periods of time that the majority of members were in fact not volunteers. All mid and senior non-commissioned offices and all officers who remain in service are de facto volunteers. The Army in Vietnam had a majority of volunteers—some perhaps motivated to enlist by a pending draft.)

The Future Threat That Demands Excellence in Leadership

Our military leaders well understand that the nation faces a variety of novel threats. From the wrecking-ball smash of a small nuclear weapon triggered among communication satellites—the resulting electromagnetic pulses shutting down perhaps our entire electrical grid—to the poisoning of water sources, the planting of toxins, the small nuclear device in an urban area, a cluster of small bomb-carrying drones headed for the

---

[62] CSIS, *American Military Culture in the Twenty-First Century*, 38. This report describes lingering challenges to forging an effective military in a democracy necessarily sensitive to political, social, and economic issues. It presents strategic overviews along with detailed data from surveys of more than 12,500 members of the armed forces. The findings seem as relevant in 2017 as in 2000. Also available at http://www.csis.org.

Mall of America, to a cell of suicide bombers with eyes on the Super Bowl, physical and perhaps other existential threats are here.

Analyzing our mission portfolio and computing resource levels essential for their completion are in themselves tasks of enormous complexity, made more complex by a system of national budgeting not famous for strategic coherence or inherent consistency. Senior military leaders must articulate an objective rationale for particular defense expenditures. In this case, "objective" includes without bias toward parent service or organization. They must build sound relationships with civilian leaders in and outside of government, some of whom have never conversed with a professional soldier.

As of this writing, defense percentage as part of the national budget moves lower while costs for people and machines rise. The requirement for deploying military forces around the globe does not greatly diminish. Both the Army and Navy may soon be at a size not seen since 1940 unless major additional funding comes to the rescue. The increasing public appetite for a variety of social services, particularly those that derive from an aging population and the debilitating effects of a sedentary lifestyle, will strain the national pocketbook. For military leaders, this means efficiently managing resources while making a persuasive case for a correct balance between missions and resources. There is no absolute right size of active or reserve forces. The size and mix must be based on the relationship between assigned missions and the long-term resources needed to prepare for and perform those missions. We can draft a private tomorrow but it takes a decade to develop a platoon sergeant, and longer to field a new generation of helicopters.

Future Cultural Adaptation

Twenty-first-century realities may dictate severe modification of aspects of traditional military culture while preserving the fundamental values of the professional soldier. There are patriotic, intelligent, overweight, excessively tattooed young people more than willing to sign an enlistment contract, serve under the Uniform Code of Military Justice, become innovative cyber-warriors, and engage in exciting missions. It may no longer be necessary for all soldiers to be trained as marksmen or required to run two miles or climb a wall. Being a non-tactical specialist would require the discipline and commitment of the conventional soldier but perhaps without the need to live in barracks, practice dismounted drill, or in some cases wear a uniform.

We recognize that technology often introduces changes in unrelated activities. The bicycle changed marriage patterns in England, piped water destroying women's well-centered social gatherings in Egyptian villages, and the Pill and cell phones changing everything everywhere. Among innovations, the biggest impact on the practice of leadership may be communication devices. Coaching by cell phone or issuing orders by Skype can undermine mutual trust in an era when trust is crucial.

Leaders have to be alert as well to technology's potential for distorting information. Perceptions are broadcast worldwide within microseconds of an event. When the good soldier on a remote mountaintop at the edge of civilization sends that first spot report (that is "always wrong") that simultaneously reaches the immediate headquarters, the Pentagon, a congressman, the soldier's family, miscellaneous hackers, and cable news, awkward things can happen. Almost nothing can remain classified. This means that every leader has one additional reason for providing clear intent and nurturing mutual trust. Knowing their commander's intent and confident of their authority to act on that intent, subordinates can take appropriate action. These are traditionally desirable behaviors taking on greater importance. In this century, strategic corporals populate the landscape.

The Obligation for Upward Coaching by Military Leaders

One conspicuous product of unfamiliarity with ground warfare and its air support is the preposterous—if understandable—expectation to wage war without collateral damage. How all soldiers would like to destroy only the bad guys. Whether or not any tendency at the political level to impose unrealistic tactical constraints can be leavened by education or enhanced mutual trust remains to be seen. Military leaders must take the initiative in resolving what is not a civil–military issue but an educational deficiency, sometimes on both sides. That responsibility for informing both the public and the elected officials can be met in great part by explaining at every opportunity the realities of warfare and the rationale for the ethics of the profession.

Tactics in most institutions are more fun than strategy. But most corporate board members and senior executives—except perhaps former members of the legal staff—have spent time on the production line before they moved to the corner office. This is not true typically of the appointed officials of the Department of Defense, except in instances—as of the time of this writing-- where former military officers have moved to senior appointed positions. The lack of military experience among legislators and appointed officials will become increasingly common as percentages of the national population with military experience dwindle.

The question of who is ultimately in charge has never been questioned in the American military tradition: an historical rarity. But the dividing line between legitimate oversight of operations and dysfunctional meddling deserves the more rigorous study it may be receiving. Such review will benefit all parties. Here again we are in the complex domain of institutional cultural analysis.

The increasing distance between military and civilian cultures (an inevitable artifact of an all-volunteer force), including the notion of the military as a family business that finds more and more recruits coming from military families, highlights the need for military leaders to coach their nonmilitary colleagues while also listening and learning from them. Even when the operational practicality for not bypassing the chain of command is understood, the impatience for results, push of global news media, and need to feel in control can fuel the temptation for seniors both military and civilian to micromanage. Technology is the tool, ignorance of military operations is the facilitator, risk-avoidance protecting a career is a helper, and mistrust is a player in the scenario where generals direct platoons and political leaders give orders to ship captains.

At what point and how the uniformed military leader asserts a thoughtful defense of the professional military ethic is another question with few definitive answers. Awareness and discussion of the topic, with affirmation of the notion that disagreement disloyalty, should not be confined to military circles.

Resigning in protest over policy decisions made by civilian or military leaders has never been seen as acceptable behavior for leaders in the American military. The point at which an officer concludes there is an ethical situation demanding resignation on principle remains also one of enormous complexity. One guideline for making such a momentous decision is to be certain of the true basis of the dilemma. What is in fact the driving factor in the issue at hand? A particularly difficult decision would arise when a leader believes that policies themselves create unethical reality where operating units would be unnecessarily subjected to persistent unjustified danger.

Leaders in the twenty-first century need to master their art, continue their learning, and be willing to modify culture while unwilling to compromise professional or personal ethics. Their sacred obligation to safeguard traditional standards arises not because they are "traditional," but because they produce results. They must adapt, listen, experiment, and create climates that attract and motivate the brightest and the best. We now place concurrent demands on our leaders: do not change with the times, and change with the times. Thankfully, there are institutional precedents for coping successfully with such a challenge.

Notes from the Notes of Part 7

Appendix A

Leadership Assessment Tools

1. The Leader Behavior Preferences Worksheet (LBP)

This survey was designed for use in the division commander studies in OIF and OEF. It has been used since in a few related informal reviews. It was received well by participants for its clarity and relevance. The utility of such surveys in enhancing organizational effectiveness depends greatly on the interest of institutional leaders. Somebody in authority must distill the essence, broadcast the lessons learned, and, when appropriate, insert them in doctrine.

The survey heading is important: *Behaviors that create a command climate that supports operational excellence and also motivate competent people to continue their military service.* It is designed to attend to the command responsibilities of both today and tomorrow.

...reate a command climate that supports operational excellence
...te competent people to continue their military service

...behavior

...ly to new situations and requirements.
2. ... and employs current Army and Joint doctrine.
3. Keeps cool under pressure.
4. Knows how and when to involve others in decision-making.
5. Clearly explains missions, standards, and priorities.
6. Sees the big picture; provides context and perspective.
7. Sets high standards without a "zero defects" mentality.
8. Encourages initiative and welcomes new ideas.
9. Backs up subordinates; confronts the boss if necessary.
10. Is trustworthy; keeps promises or explains why he can't.
11. Employs units in accordance with their capabilities.
12. Can handle "bad news."
13. Gets out of the headquarters and visits the troops.
14. Coaches and gives useful feedback to subordinates.
15. Sets a high ethical tone; demands honest reporting.
16. Will share the risks and hardships of his soldiers.
17. Knows how to delegate and not "micromanage."
18. Is consistent and predictable in behavior.
19. Shows respect and consideration for others of any rank.
20. Puts mission and people ahead of his or her own career.
21. Is approachable; listens to questions and suggestions.
22. Can make tough, sound decisions on time.
23. Shares the limelight; gives due credit to others.
24. Senses unproductive policies and makes prompt adjustments.
25. Builds and supports teamwork within staff and among units.
26. Holds people accountable for their actions and results.
27. Is more interested in doing good than looking good.
28. Is fair; doesn't play favorites with units or people.
29. Is positive, encouraging, and realistically optimistic.

2. Assessment of Power Distribution in Organizations (APDO)

The APDO comes from the *Systems Leadership Program* at the Center for Creative Leadership (CCL). Each of the items represents a policy or technique that should enhance appropriate distribution of power or authority through the organization. It is in itself a teaching tool. It reminds us of policies that can introduce true empowerment throughout the organization.

The APDO is best used with the Predicted Response Comparison (PRC) model first mentioned in Note 12. The true test of an empowered organization is whether or not desirable policies coming from on high are in fact in place and supported two or three levels below. The APDO could be given to three levels, with a prediction of how the levels below and above will respond. A bit complex, it is worth the effort *if* indeed the senior executives are truly interested in each echelon playing its proper role. The executives who participated in the program and collected data from their organizations believed it hit the mark. It seems unique as an instrument.

Each item describes one component of an appropriately decentralized climate. Respondents evaluate the importance of each item on a scale as from 1 = disagree to 5 = strongly agree, and for importance from 1 = not important to 5 = very important. It is useful to spend time discussing the instrument in detail before its use. Considering the meaning and importance of each question in open session contributes to its utility.

		Agreement	Importance
APDO Part 1. Reinforcing organizational vision, trust, and values			
1.	**Our organizational climate is rational, positive, and supportive.** (Things make sense around here.)		
2.	**We have clear goals and priorities.** (Some things are higher priority than others.)		
3.	**Our organization is serious about honesty and integrity.** (We don't tolerate cheating by anybody for any purpose.)		
4.	**Our leaders understand that inherently good programs may have disastrous side effects.** (Our leaders understand the whole picture.)		
5.	**You don't have to compromise your integrity and come up with phony statistics in our unit.** (You can tell it like it is, explain it, and go on.)		
6.	**Our senior leaders don't have a "zero defects" mentality that prompts dishonesty and frustration.** (They recognize what is possible and not.)		
7.	**Our senior leaders exemplify the espoused values of the organization.** (Their actions are consistent with their expectations and promises.)		
APDO Part 2. Developing and respecting the legitimate authority of subordinate echelons			
8.	**Our leaders trust subordinates and expect them to use good judgment.** (People are treated as trustworthy and responsible adults.)		
9.	**Our leaders show their intent to empower subordinates and solve problems at the lowest possible level.** (They know they cannot do it all.)		

10.	**Our higher headquarters understands that too many rules hamper necessary initiative.** (They understand local initiative must be protected.)		
11.	**We have authority to make decisions at our level, and our leaders will back us up.** (Our leaders don't interfere without good reason.)		
12.	**Our leaders understand that everybody deserves a warning order.** (We get advance notice whenever it is possible and are not jerked around.)		
13.	**Our leaders typically solicit input before changing the rules of the game.** (We are consulted when possible about matters in our area of expertise.)		
14.	**Developing subordinates—coaching and ensuring training—receives attention in our unit.** (We get regular feedback and go to school on time.)		

APDO Part 3. Providing open, convenient channels for communication			
15.	**We share good ideas, knowing that what helps one part of the organization helps us all.** (We don't hide ideas or keep info to ourselves.)		
16.	**New policy or new schedules are given first to leaders to pass along.** (Subordinates look to their immediate leader for critical information.)		
17.	**We have reliable ways of letting leaders know of policies that seem "dumb."** (There are convenient methods for highlighting dysfunctional policies.)		
18.	**Systems for measuring and reporting are open to constructive change.** (Methods for addressing concerns about reporting systems are in place.)		
19.	**Review and analysis sessions are opportunities for discussion and education, not "gotcha" exercises.** (We keep statistics in perspective.)		
20.	**This organization is open to new ideas.** (Leaders invite and listen to ideas.)		
21.	**We have a reputable system for assessing and reviewing the climate.**		

3. Assessment of Selected Aspects of the Command Climate (ACC)

1	2		3	4		5	6
Marginal			Satisfactory			Exceeds expectations	

A. A strong, healthy focus on mission accomplishment.

Your view	1	2	3	4	5	6
CG's view	1	2	3	4	5	6

B. Clarity of standards, goals, and priorities.

Your view	1	2	3	4	5	6
CG's view	1	2	3	4	5	6

C. A reliable, timely, open flow of key information.

Your view	1	2	3	4	5	6
CG's view	1	2	3	4	5	6

D. An appreciation for initiative and innovation.

Your view	1	2	3	4	5	6
CG's view	1	2	3	4	5	6

E. Consideration for the well-being of people.

Your view	1	2	3	4	5	6
CG's view	1	2	3	4	5	6

F. A prevailing sense of mutual trust and confidence.

Your view	1	2	3	4	5	6
CG's view	1	2	3	4	5	6

On the next page are the comparative responses from two of the questions using the Predicted Results Comparison (PRC) technique. The division commander rated each aspect of the climate and others also rated it. Further, the division commander predicted how others would rate and others predicted how he would rate. Participants included the four commanding generals (CGs) and 107 of their subordinates. (Commanders and deputy commanders: 37; Division Staff: 59. Grades O-6, O-5, and O-4.) Other breakouts for analysis were by grade and position.

An example of the results from comparative perspectives is shown below. They include averages of three of the six ACC elements, items A, C, and E.

Averages moderate differences and do not reveal the spectrum of responses. Here we see a pattern of no meaningful differences in response pattern in item A, and an interesting spread in item C. In all cases, the CG was less positive in assessment than his subordinates.

Why the boss differs significantly from the response pattern of subordinates is worthy of examination. If the boss is consistently more positive, it could mean he is out of touch. If he is typically less positive, a phenomenon common with transformational leaders, that could indicate high expectations or self-modesty. Major differences deserve thought.

(Scale: 1-2 = marginal to 5-6 = Exceeds expectations.)	3.2	3.4	3.6	3.8	4.0	4.2	4.4	4.6	4.8	5.0 +
A. A strong, healthy focus on mission accomplishment.										
—How the CGs rated (4.50)							■			
—How the CGs predicted others would rate (4.75)								■		
—How others rated (5.01)										■
—How others predicted the CG would rate (5.01)										■
C. A reliable, timely, open flow of key information.										
—How the CGs rated (3.25)	■									
—How the CGs predicted others would rate (3.75)			■							
—How others rated (4.22)						■				
—How others predicted the CG would rate (4.53)							■			
E. Consideration for the well-being of people.										
—How the CGs rated (4.00)				■						
—How the CGs predicted others would rate (4.50)								■		
—How others rated (5.08)										■
—How others predicted the CG would rate (5.21)										■

4. A More Definitive Climate Survey

My preference is for a relatively short survey like this. It minimizes administration and can decrease participant discouragement. Even this length, which expands on the basic elements described in Note 27, can provide a reasonably definitive analysis of climate factors. A couple additional items could be added by the local commander to address any immediate concerns.

Item	Statement	SD	D	A	SA
1	I am proud to serve in America's armed forces.				
2	We have high standards of discipline in this unit.				
3	I can trust members of my team to do their share of the work.				
4	My job is important in accomplishing our mission.				
5	We have clear goals and priorities.				
6	My immediate leader lets me know how well I am doing my job.				
7	Military traditions and values mean a lot to members of this unit.				
8	People are treated fairly in this unit regardless of gender or race.				
9	We have the resources we need to do our job properly.				
10	We have a lot of teamwork going on in this unit.				
11	Our leaders put mission first and their own careers second.				
12	Our leaders can make tough, sound decisions on time.				
13	Our leaders do not let their personal friendships interfere with their duties.				
14	Leaders in this unit are open to new ideas.				
15	I can do my job well and have time for family/personal life when not deployed.				
16	You can "tell it like it is" in this unit; we don't hide bad news.				
17	Senior leaders in this organization exemplify high standards on and off duty.				

18	If I have a personal or health problem, I am comfortable asking for help.				
19	Leaders in this unit do not "micromanage"; they understand "mission type orders."				
20	We do not have drug or alcohol abuse problems in this unit.				
21	I am well trained to do my job as a member of this unit.				
22	There is no sexual harassment or bullying in this unit.				
23	In a tough situation, this unit can be depended on to perform well.				
24	To be added by the local commander related to the specific environment.				

5. The Systems Leadership Report Card (SLRC)

This survey, also known as Comparative Perceptions of the Organizational Climate (CPOC), was designed to measure the comparative views of the leader with peers, subordinates, or other informed observers on broad elements of the climate. It provides a broad overview of perceptions. Deciding which elements were most difficult to change prompted useful discussions of organizational culture.

Item 17 on the overall climate needs agreement on definition prior to taking the survey as to what "organization" is being discussed. The instrument can be scored on some convenient scale—from 1 = great to 6 = substandard.

	Item	Self	Others
1.	Value Reinforcement (organizational values clarified and nourished routinely)		
2.	Vision (understanding what the organization can and should be)		
3.	Commitment (dedication to organizational mission and values)		
4.	Goals and Priorities (knowing clearly the performance goals and task priorities)		
5.	Integrity and Trust (a prevailing sense of honest dealing and mutual trust)		
6.	Latitude/Power (appropriate latitude and authority in doing the job)		
7.	Open Channels (systematic and informal communications up, down, and across)		
8.	Policy Coherence (policies and practices congruent with goals and priorities)		
9.	Measurement and Feedback (effectiveness assessed and reported reliably)		
10.	Team-Building (cooperative group work routinely supported)		
11.	Performance Appraisal/Reward (individual performance assessed and rewarded)		
12.	Personal Development (plans and programs for growing future leaders)		
13.	Resource Accessibility (essential materials or funds obtainable)		
14.	Junk Destruction (opportunities to eliminate dumb stuff and whitewash)		
15.	Pace and Stress (reasonable levels of activity and demands for the situation)		
16.	Humor (timely injections of lightheartedness and fun)		
17.	The Climate Overall (that part of the organization meaningful to you and subordinates)		

6. Climate Survey for Staffs

This instrument includes items that address the typical concerns of staff members. It is most relevant at brigade and higher levels. It could provide results indicating excellence to be celebrated as well as possible unethical or toxic leadership that deserves follow-up.

	Statement	Strongly disagree to strongly agree					
		SD	D	-?	+?	A	SA
1.	In my section, our goals and priorities are clear.						
2.	Plans and schedules relevant to my work are provided well in advance.						
3.	I receive constructive feedback on my methods and results.						
4.	I can make appropriate contributions to the staff decision-making process.						
5.	We have effective communication with members of subordinate staffs.						
6.	Staff leaders make timely decisions; they don't pass the buck.						
7.	We can take reasonable risks on this staff; no "zero defects" mentality here.						
8.	Our leaders show respect and consideration for others regardless of rank.						
9.	We have personnel and other resources required to do our job properly.						
10.	Teamwork is encouraged and supported in this staff; we share information.						
11.	Our leaders hold people accountable for their actions and results.						
12.	Deadlines for taskings are typically reasonable and based on legitimate needs.						
13.	Our leaders do not play favorites with people or subordinate units.						

14.	I can do my job well and have time for family/personal life when not deployed.						
15	You can "tell it like it is" in this staff; we don't hide bad news.						
16.	My tour on this staff will contribute to my professional development.						
17.	If I have a personal or health problem, I am comfortable seeking help.						
18.	We do not receive conflicting guidance from different senior leaders.						
19.	We do not have drug, alcohol, or sexual-harassment problems on this staff.						
20.	Our meetings are usually on time, well-organized, and productive.						
21.	I am encouraged to ask for clarification if mission guidance is not clear to me.						
22.	Senior leaders in this organization exemplify the standards of our profession.						
23.	We focus on substantive matters, not "show and tell" projects.						
24	Leaders on this staff know how to delegate and not "micromanage."						
25.	Our senior leaders take time to coach and mentor.						
26.	Everything considered morale on this staff is high.						
27.	To be added by the local commander.						
28.	To be added by the local commander.						

7. The Leader Relationships Map (LRM)

Leaders differ in the manner in which they interact with particular subordinates. A component of that difference is the degree of "reciprocal influence" between the leader and subordinate—the state of mutual respect, cooperation, commitment, communication, and trust that is often manifested in capacity to influence decisions, actions, or attitudes of one on the other. Some refer to this as *connectedness*.

Some leaders have a relatively small number of close working relationships, preferring more formal, somewhat impersonal styles to influence outcomes. Others have close ties with many of their subordinates. A position in the inner circles of this graphic would suggest a close relationship, a position in the outer rings a more impersonal relationship. The placement of a collection of individuals in these circles reveals a pattern of perceived reciprocal influence that says something about the leader's style and the kind of "team" that has been created. Why individuals imagine themselves in one ring and their peers in another could shed light on the climate in general, on mutual trust, and on the quality of communication.

Instructions for completion of this exercise: Please consider all subordinates who work directly for the commanding general (CG), including you. Then place those names (or positions, if you prefer) on the circles, indicating the degree of reciprocal influence that you believe exists between these individuals and the CG.

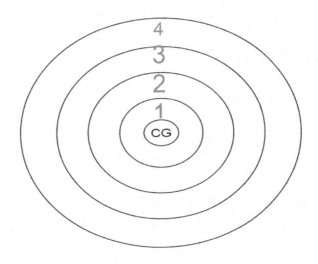

When each individual indicates, privately, in which circle he believes himself to be situated in relative closeness to the boss, and also indicates where he sees others, that effort in itself—when discussed with a savvy coach—is useful. If permission has been given to discuss these individual perceptions with the boss in the center of the circle, the boss can gain unique insights.

An example of the use of the Predicted Results Comparison model (PRC) can be shown with the LRM below. Again, the LRM requires a mature and trusting environment for its administration. If such a climate prevails, it offers a formidable method of enhancing self-awareness and strengthening teamwork, disclosing any perceptions of favoritism.

The boss (B) has indicated where the nine key subordinates reside in terms of distance/access/influence from him. Then, in this example, an average of the nine subordinates' views (O for others) is shown in comparison. An even more intimate and precise discussion could be generated when individuals compare their perceptions with those of the boss. Boss versus average is a safer, less personal or emotional technique.

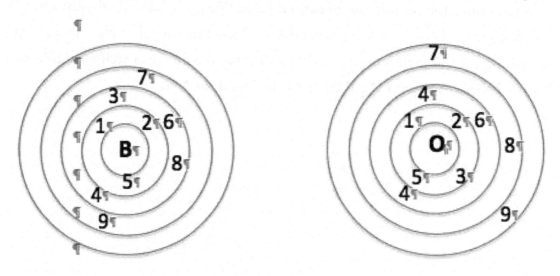

Here are typical positions that might be included: 1. chief of staff; 2. deputy #1; 3. deputy #2; 4. inspector general; 5. legal advisor; 6. major commander A; 7. major commander B; 8.

senior liaison officer; 9. attached major unit commander. In this (manufactured) situation, the boss has a pretty good feel for levels of access/influence of most of his relationships. But outsiders see a stronger relationship between him and the Inspector general (4) and major commander A (6) than exists from the boss's perspective. The boss senses that the senior liaison officer (8) and the attached major unit commander (9) feel a bit left out, but in fact all participants see them as even more remote from the boss.

The operable question is how both the boss and others will use this to enhance organizational effectiveness. In most cases, it would be prudent to have a facilitator lead the discussion of cause, effect, and desirable initiatives.

8. Staff Performance Feedback Form (SPFF)

This form is the only survey instrument included in this book that has not been field-tested. It was designed to fill a particular need in the staff tune-up process. It is a multi-observer assessment of how the staff is meeting the needs of major constituents: subordinate and peer staffs. There have always been informal assessments ("They get the word out fast," "You can never get a straight answer," "You never know who to contact," etc.) However, most often there are no convenient means of providing coherent, regular feedback from users other than the senior leaders of the staff itself. That feedback is often limited to whether or not the staff product is on time, in the proper format, and coherent.

There is no staff—just as there is no large organization—that is internally consistent in the quality of work. While the personnel section of a staff may get glowing reviews, the logistics section may be seen as less than productive. So perhaps the best use of the SPFF in a large staff would be in assessing a particular staff section or directorate. The fact that feedback is invited using the SPFF would in itself be a potentially productive step in inter-staff relations. The SPFF and its explanatory notes would be distributed within the command and to outside agencies that work with the staff. Its use could be optional or a part of periodic reviews. The fact that an SPFF exists would be an indicator of institutional interest in perceptions of staff effectiveness. (The Joint Staff in the Pentagon had initiated recently some individual and team assessments.)

Staff Performance Feedback Form (SPFF)		
	Item	**Comments**
1.	We have a convenient point of contact for communication with that staff.	
2.	We have an honest, candid exchange of information with that staff.	
3.	That staff understands our needs.	
4.	That staff tailors its products and considers our deadlines.	
5.	That staff responds to requests in a timely manner.	
6.	That staff is open to suggestions about its operation.	
7.	That staff provides suggestions for improving our operation.	
8.	Morale on that staff looks pretty good from our perspective.	
9.	To be added by the local commander.	
10.	To be added by the local commander.	

Appendix B

Potential Commander Assessment Process (PCAP)

This Appendix uses a future scenario to offer one solution to the institutional challenge of selecting the best available individuals to lead critical elements of the organization. Selecting leaders is simply the most important internal function of the military institution.

Our history has confirmed the general effectiveness of military selection systems. However, there are lingering, legitimate concerns about a system whose ranks include some toxic or incompetent leaders. Further, there are significant numbers of selected leaders who survive but are incapable of building high-performing organizations. While a variety of factors influence institutional performance, nothing compares to the contributions of leaders. The perceived quality of the selection process itself contributes greatly to perceptions of the quality of the institution. Frustration with selection processes may well have contributed to the loss of some high potential young leaders.

Leaders at the battalion-command level (lieutenant colonels in charge of units or sections) are especially powerful. They are the subject of this discussion. Those lieutenant colonels have unique opportunities to set the climate that inspires or discourages talented subordinates. Because a high percentage of future opportunities for promotion are from the pool of those selected for battalion-level command, it is sort of the key to the kingdom.

Expenses for leader selection and development, and for continuing officer education, are not trivial in current budgets. Yet in perspective they remain low in proportion to their impact on organizational effectiveness. In the imaginary scenario that follows, describing the *Potential Commander Assessment Program,* its methods and history, the PCAP budget would be a fraction of the average spent annually over the last decade on selecting handguns, camouflage patterns, and ready-to-eat meals.

The Interview

2 April, 2029

Camp Grant, Virginia

Reporter: Colonel Alden, I am Ashley from the News. Thanks for taking time to discuss the history of the Potential Commander Assessment Program. Or the PCAP as you call it.

COL A: Our pleasure. This is out tenth anniversary and we are pleased to discuss it.

Reporter: How did it start, and why, and what exactly do you do? Later I will ask your view of its contribution to our Army.

COL A: We began in 2019 as an effort to compliment traditional methods of selecting lieutenant colonels for command positions in all parts of our Army. We would take advantage of all available techniques to enhance the selection process. Some of these selected lieutenant colonels would serve in tactical battalions, some in installation management, some in technical formations. All those positions require good leadership in addition to technical expertise.

Reporter: Why do you focus on lieutenant colonels? How about captains or generals?

COL A: Our selection systems attempt to get the right people at all levels. But lieutenant colonel commands are unique in the hierarchy. They link the point of the spear and the higher organization. They are close enough to know their soldiers as individuals, but high enough to require a sophisticated view of the institution. They set the climate and the personal example that directly, daily, affects the life of those in the organization. They are the first level of command that has a staff of some sort, and the level that has to absorb all the directives and policies of higher echelons, sort them out, and make them work. To the junior officers in particular they directly represent our Army.

Reporter: Who are your students and how are they selected?

COL A: Our students are majors who will be available for selection for lieutenant colonel commands in a couple years. They had volunteered to enter the course. Then their career managers in personnel headquarters, and I hate to use the term "manager," reviewed their record. If it indicates that they have a reasonable chance of being selected for battalion-level command they are accepted. The major's current commander may add a comment regarding the appropriateness of the course for that individual, and that comment is considered by the personnel folks in their decision.

Reporter: Does a major have to attend the PCAP to be selected for battalion-level command?

COL A: That is an interesting question. When the course was first proposed, it was a totally voluntary sort of an add-on that might help the individual and the Army make a better choice about suitability for command. But soon it became apparent that either the course was contributing to selection success or that those volunteering were the cream of the crop. The word was out that attending the course seemed to improve chances. In any case, now it is rare that a major is selected for command who has not been through the course. There are many graduates of PCAP who are not selected for battalion-level command simply because of limited slots available. We try to admit those who have indicated a considerable potential, but relying too heavily on the limited formal records of majors with perhaps 6-8 years in responsible positions was one of the problems in the first place. If we had the resources we might use it for all majors since it provides a unique gift of feedback about intellectual, emotional, and physical fitness unequalled in our universe. But it's expensive and we need to make choices and we will make some number of mistakes in those choices. Overall, we believe that with our input promotion boards now make fewer selection mistakes.

Reporter: How relatively good or bad was the conventional system?

COL A: Well, it was good enough to win WWII and provide formidable forces in Korea, Vietnam, and post 9/11 engagements. But our soldiers and our countrymen deserved even better. A reasonable guess might be that back in 2015 perhaps four out of ten battalion-level commanders were remarkably good, three or four were adequate, and two or three should never have been selected for the position. Just my estimates. You will hear different numbers based on who you talk to! We should be able to select and get six of ten remarkably good and the other four almost that good. The talent has always been there. The trick is finding it.

Reporter: This is your tenth year. Has the course been a success? Has it been a better screening mechanism? Has it been worth the price—I note some expensive facilities here at Camp Grant.

COL A: Evaluating educational or selection outcomes is not an exact science. A variety of factors are responsible for any discernible change in an institution. But we think there are indicators reflecting our impact. First, over the last seven years surveys show improved morale, reduction in absenteeism and accidents, higher re-enlistment rates, and a slowing of officers leaving the Army after their obligatory tour is up. This is particularly true for the four-year ROTC scholarship and West Point officers. There may be other factors intervening, but during the last decade there have not been dramatic changes in deployment rates or costs of living or civilian employment opportunities or military funding or public support of the military or military pay and allowances that might cause such change. These positive changes have been in both troop units and in other agencies. One particular data point: those who have received our highest grade and then been selected for battalion-level command have been without exception successful in that command. Almost 100% of those who received our highest grade have been selected for command. And we give only three grades: A, B, or C.

Reporter: What do the apparently better leaders get from the course?

COL A: An excellent question. We are both a selection and a development activity. So far in history there have been few perfect leaders. Our records show that none have come through our course so far! But as we say, "You don't need to be sick to get better!" We believe we make a meaningful contribution by assisting in development, by letting all leaders know more about strengths and weaknesses, and how to grow as a leader and a person. Our graduates give us high marks, even in cases where their news is not all good.

Reporter: How does your course work? What information do prospective candidates have about the course before their two weeks in residence?

COL A: Let me give you a copy of the information letter we provide majors who will enter the course.

Reporter: Do you think you have identified all the potential toxic leaders?

COL A: Surely not. Our methods are not foolproof. And a few well-balanced thirty-five-year-old majors will somehow morph into disgruntled colonels or generals. But very few of those receiving an A or B grade will do that, because we focus on their hard-wiring that changes little over time. And we are much more concerned with identifying potential toxics than fingering future super-stars. But helping all. Hopefully, a toxic leader will soon be a rarity in our Army.

Reporter: Will you accidentally rate some of the majors C when they really deserve a B or even an A?

COL A: Unfortunately, in spite of our best efforts, probably yes. And remember we are not saying they are C in life, nor are they typically potentially toxic. They are just C in the command selection process. We make that clear to all concerned. We do remain more concerned with the best interest of the troops in general than with the career of any individual in particular.

Reporter: Colonel, thanks for your time, courtesy, and candor. You have an impressive program. Anything else you would like to add?

COL A: Just thanks for the opportunity to share information on this important effort!

·········

Dear Major Cameron-Hudson,

On behalf of Colonel Alden, commander of Army PCAP activities, I welcome you to the PCAP program! Your two weeks in residence here with the other twenty-three members of Class 29-4, will commence on 6 September. That provides about four months for planning. If your unit deploys or other operational needs intervene, we can reschedule.

Let me outline the program. Some of this you knew when you applied, but I want to add details. We assume that sometime in the next two years you will be considered by the command selection board.

After completing this two-week program, you will receive a summary grade of A, B, or C. You will have the option of making that grade available to the command selection board. The board will consider that grade along with your performance record and other materials in your personnel file. You will control the distribution of all results of our assessment.

Here are some specifics:

- The purpose of the exercise is to provide you, and if you see fit the Army via the selection board, with data about your potential and development as a leader.
- At the completion of the program you will receive a comprehensive summary of our assessment, along with the summary grade.

- The summary grade is defined as follows:
    - A. Apparently well qualified for battalion-level command. (So far, 35% rate.)
    - B. Apparently qualified for battalion-level command. (So far, 45% rate.)
    - C. Questionably qualified for battalion-level command. (So far, 20% rate.)

- Selection boards are briefed on how the grade was determined, what it means, and that no conclusion should be reached about any candidates for command who did not choose to attend PCAP, or who attended and did not provide the board with a grade.
- Each class at PCAP has twenty-four participants. They are majors of the same career path who will eventually be competing for selection for command.
- This is not a boot camp. But it is physically and intellectually demanding. It requires no specific preparation other than the completion of the paperwork mentioned. Bring dress and field uniforms, a good pair of running shoes, your favorite boots, and some casual civilian clothes. Leave all of your electronic devices at home. Having one here is basis for dismissal from the class, and that will be a matter of official record.
- The name of the game is assessment. You will be monitored and evaluated and tested and questioned from the moment you arrive through the evening social the day prior to your departure. Understandably, you and your classmates may be anxious. However, be assured that our processes are safe, tested, monitored, and never embarrassing. You may have friends who have participated in an earlier PCAP. (Yes, we change the details and the exercises from class to class.)
- We do not grade on a curve. You will not be competing directly with your classmates. You will be compared to carefully designed standards. (For example, all members of your class could receive a grade of A or a grade of C.) This is kind of a "cooperate and graduate" environment.
- Our staff are highly trained and experienced. A few are active duty members of a variety of specialties. We have staff who are clinical and cognitive psychologists,

medical officers, sports medicine specialists, information technologists. Some are former faculty members from the School of Advanced Military Studies at Leavenworth or the War College. Some were observer-controllers at a National Training Centers or lane-graders at Ranger School.

- In preparation for PCAP you were asked to identify ten subordinates and six peers who have served with you for at least six months in an assignment prior to your current one. They will be asked to complete the two behavioral questionnaires that you also completed. (Neither you nor they will know if a particular individual's input was considered by our staff since we will select at random eight of the ten subordinates and four of the six peers. You may inform them of your request that they participate if you choose. In any case they will receive information on the purpose of the exercise and instructions on confidentiality. If one of your requested participants declines to complete the questionnaires we will ask you to select another candidate.)

- We will evaluate various aspects of brainpower, tenacity, physical and emotional fitness, and teamwork. There will be written exercises, and small group exercises where your behavior under mid-levels of stress will be observed. Some exercises are presented through virtual reality and interactive devices. You will act as a battalion commander in a twelve-hour computer-assisted war game suited to your particular specialty.

- Your class will be divided into four teams of six. You and your teammates will compete with the other three teams in orienteering (maps and compasses, no electronics), volleyball, dismounted drill (yes!), weapons competition, a dune-buggy race, the development of a traditional brigade operations order, and the employment of drones to assess an enemy encampment. We collect data on both methods and results of these competitions.

- Each morning and evening we will collect a blood sample; you will wear a heart monitor for a few hours in some activities; and we will conduct a brain scan. (You will take home a remarkable mix of useful information on your heath.)

- Prior to your arrival, we ask you to compose a personal philosophy of leadership using a format we will provide. We ask also that you describe in detail in two or three pages what you would prefer to be doing over the next ten years of your career.

- We use a few peer assessments. We will ask that you prioritize various strengths of your classmates. (The staff will worry about addressing weaknesses!)

- If at any time during the assessment weeks you decide not to continue, you will be released immediately with no record of that decision. (In courses in the last nine years we have not had a single participant request to leave for other than health or family emergency reasons. We have, however, had a few change their mind about attending after reading this outline of the course.)

- On the final day of the program you will have a three-hour feedback session. That staff member will provide all of the test results and observations, with suggestions for reinforcing your strengths and repairing your weaknesses. You will find that session comfortable, interesting, and productive. Whatever your future career, these data will be helpful in your personal and career-development. This information is confidential. It is yours to keep and use as you see fit. Our staff members do not leak to anybody.

- Many who receive a C grade, and a few who receive a B grade, conclude upon reflection they are better suited to make a contribution and achieve career success and personal satisfaction elsewhere in our Army than in command positions. We believe our stimulating such insight is a significant contribution.

- We on the staff hold after-action reviews on our performance after each class, conduct our assessments in compliance with professional protocols, and do our very best to create for you a reliable, useful assessment.
We look forward to your joining us in a few months!

Sincerely, Major Adrian Bennett

Appendix C
References Cited

Aslakson, Eric, and Richard T. Brown. 2016. "Staff Colonels Are Army's Innovative Engines." *Army* (December).

Bass, B. M. et al. 1987. "Transformation Leadership and the Falling Dominoes Effect." *Group & Organization Studie*s 12 (1).

Bass, B. M., and B. J. Avolio. 2000. *Platoon Readiness as a Function of Leadership, Platoon, and Company Cultures. Final Report.* Washington, DC: U.S. Army Research Institute for the Behavioral and Social Sciences.

Bekoft, Marc, and Jessica Pierce. 2009. *Wild Justice: The Moral Lives of Animals.* Chicago: University of Chicago Press.

Berkun, Mitchell M. et. al. 1952. "Experimental Studies of Psychological Stress in Man." *Psychological Monographs General and Applied*, vol. 76-15. American Psychological Association, Inc.

Botelho, Elena Lytkina et. al. 2017. "What Sets Successful CEOs Apart." In Harvard Business Review, May-June, 70-77.

Campbell, David P. 1995. "The Psychological Profiles of Brigadier Generals: Warmongers or Decisive Warriors?" In *Assessing Individual Differences in Human Behavior*, edited by D. Lubinski and R. V. Dawis, 145–175. Palo Alto, CA: Davies-Black.

Center for Strategic and International Studies. 2000. *American Military Culture in the Twenty-First Century: A Report of the CSIS International Security Program.* Washington, DC: CSIS. Also at http://www.csis.org.

Chaleff, Ira. 1995. *The Courageous Follower: Standing Up to and For Our Leaders.* San Francisco: Berrett-Koehler Publishers, Inc. (2d ed. 2003.)

Chappelow, Craig T. 2004. "360-Degree Feedback." In *The Center for Creative Leadership Handbook of Leader Development, Second Edition.* San Francisco: Jossey-Bass and Center for Creative Leadership.

Cook, Martin J. 2008. "Revolt of the Generals: A Case Study in Professional Ethics." In Parameters: U.S. Army War College Quarterly: (Spring) 4-15.

Deane, Anthony E. 2016. *Ramadi Unclassified: A Roadmap to Peace in the Most Dangerous City in Iraq.* Bay Village, Ohio: Praetorian Books.

Drath, Winfred H. 1993. *Why Leaders Have Trouble Empowering: A Theoretical Perspective Based on Concepts of Adult Development.* Greensboro, NC: Center for Creative Leadership.

Durant, Will and Ariel. 1968. *The Lessons of History.* New York: Simon and Schuster. (Paperback edition 2010.)

Edon, Dov. 1992. "Leadership and Expectations: Pygmalion Effects and Other Self-fulfilling Prophecies in Organizations." *Leadership Quarterly*, 3 (4).

Egbert, Robert L. et. al. 1958. "Fighter I: A Study of Effective and Ineffective Combat Performance." Presidio of Monterey, CA: U.S. Army Leadership Human Research Unit (March).

Gerras, Stephan, and Leonard Wong. 2016. "America's Army: Measuring Quality Soldiers and Quality Officers." Carlisle, PA: U.S. Army War College.

Headquarters, Department of the Army. 1953. *FM 22-100. Command and Leadership for the Small Unit Commander.* Washington, DC (February).

———. 1993. *ATTP 5-0.1. Army Commander and Staff Officer Guide.* Washington, DC (September).

———. 1993. *TC 25-20. A Leader's Guide to After Action Reviews.* Washington, DC (September).

———. 2012. *ADRP 6-0. Mission Command.* Washington, DC (May).

———. 2014. *Army Regulation 600-20. Army Command Policy.* Washington, DC (November).

———. 2015. *ADMP (or FM) 6-22, Leader Development.* Washington, DC (June).

Industrial College of the Armed Forces. 1997. *Strategic Leadership and Decision Making: Preparing Senior Executives for the 21st Century.* Washington, DC.

Kane, Tim. 2017 "Total Volunteer Force: Blueprint for Pentagon Personnel Reform. Summary Report." Stanford, CA: Hoover Institution. [Book, June '17.]

Jacobs, T. O. 1994. *A Guide to the Strategic Leader Development Inventory.* Washington, DC: Department of Strategy, Industrial College of the Armed Forces (ICAF).

(Now the Dwight D. Eisenhower School for National Security and Resource Strategy.)

Malone, Dandridge M. 1973. "The Prize." *Army* (March) 24–32.

Marshall, S. L. A. 1947. *Men Against Fire: The Problem of Battle Command in Future War.* Washington: Combat Forces Press, and New York: William Morrow and Company.

Matthews, Lloyd J. 2002. "The Uniformed Intellectual and His Place in the American Army." Army (July) Part I, 17-25 and (August) Part II, 31-40.

McCall, Morgan W., Michael M. Lombardo, and Ann M. Morrison. 1988. *The Lessons of Experience: How Successful Executives Develop on the Job.* New York: Simon and Schuster.

McCauley, C. D. and E. VanVelsor, eds. 2004. *Handbook of Leader Development. Second Edition.* San Francisco: John Wiley & Sons, Inc.

Myrer, Anton. *Once an Eagle.* 1968. New York: Holt, Reinhart and Winston. First paperback edition, 1970 by Dell. First Army War College edition, 1997.

Noer, David M. 2016. *Keeping Your Career on Track: Avoiding Derailment, Enriching the Work Experience, and Helping Your Organization.* Jefferson, NC: McFarland and Company.

Regins, Belle Rose. 2016. "From the ordinary to the extraordinary: High Quality mentoring relationships at work." Organizational Dynamics: 45, 228-244.

Reed, George E. 2015. *Tarnished: Toxic Leadership in the U.S. Military.* University of Nebraska: Potomac Books.

Ricks, Thomas E. 2012. *The Generals: American Military Command from World War II to Today*. New York: The Penguin Press.

Stamp, Gillian. 1988. "Longitudinal Research into Methods of Assessing Managerial Potential." Alexandria, VA: U.S. Army Research Institute for the Behavioral and Social Sciences, February.

Swain, Richard M. and Pierce, Albert C. 2017. *The Armed Forces Officer*. Washington: National Defense University Press.

Toner, James H. 1996. "Readings in Military Ethics." *Military Review* (January-February): 35-42.

Toomepuu, Juri. 1980. "Soldier Capability—Army Combat Effectiveness (SCACE) Study." Fort Benjamin Harrison, IN. U.S. Army Support Center.

Ulmer, Walter F. Jr. 1998. "Military Leadership into the 21st Century: Another "Bridge Too Far?" *Parameters: The U.S. Army War College Quarterly* XXVIII (Spring): 4–25.

———. 1999. "Military Learnings: A Practitioner's Perspective" in *Tacit Knowledge in Professional Practice*, edited by Robert J. Sternberg and Joseph A. Horvath, 59–71. Mahwah, NJ: Laurence Erlbaum Associates, Publishers.

United States Army War College. 1970. *Study on Military Professionalism*. Carlisle Barracks, PA: U.S. Army War College (30 June).

———. 1971. *Leadership for the 1970s: USAWC Study of Leadership for the Professional Soldier*. Carlisle Barracks, PA: U.S. Army War College (1 July).

———. 2004. *Leadership Lessons at Division Command Level—2004*. Carlisle Barracks, PA (5 November).

———. 2011. *Leadership Lessons at Division Command Level—2010: A Review of Division Commander Leader Behaviors and Organizational Climates in Selected Army Divisions After Nine Years of War.* Carlisle Barracks, PA: U.S. Army War College (20 January).

United States Army Combined Arms Center. 9 October 2014. *The Human Dimensions White Paper: A Framework for Optimizing Human Performance.* Fort Leavenworth, Kansas.

United States Naval Institute. 1939. *Naval Leadership With Some Hints to Junior Officers and Others. Fourth Edition.* Annapolis, Maryland: The United States Naval Institute.

U.S. Army Research Institute for the Behavioral and Social Sciences. 2000. *Platoon Readiness as a Function of Leadership, Platoon, and Company Cultures.* Washington, DC: ARI (March 31).

Wolfberg, Adrian. 2016. "When Generals Consume Intelligence: The Problems That Arise and How to Solve Them." *Intelligence and National Security* (December): 1–16.

Yammerino, F. J., and L. E. Atwater. 1993. *Understanding Self-Perception Accuracy: Implications for Human Resources Management.* Binghamton, NY: School of Management and Center for Leadership Studies, State University of New York.

Appendix D
Other Excellent Reading

Five Special Books

- *Small Unit Leadership: A Commonsense Approach* by Dandridge M. Malone (Novarto, CA: The Presidio Press, 1983). This is the best, and it's about more than small unit leadership. Mike's fundamentals fit leaders at any level, at any time, in any setting.

- *The Armed Forces Officer* from the Armed Forces Information Service (Washington, DC: Department of Defense, July 22, 1975). If American military officers need a bible, this is it. Once issued to newly commissioned Army officers, it is to military leadership what Gardner's *On Leadership* is to leadership in general. In 2017 the National Defense University published a new version by Richard Swain and Albert Pierce that brings the discussion into current focus without the memorable original text.

- *On Leadership* by John G. Gardner (New York: The Free Press, 1990). On the cover of this paperback edition, I call it "a masterpiece." I still think it is: fundamentals for leading in a free society.

- *FM (or ADP) 6-22: Leader Development* (Washington, DC: Headquarters, Department of the Army, June 2015. Also on line at https://armypubs.usarmy.mil/doctrine/index/html). This Army Field Manual is an impressive, comprehensive, up-to-date document. It covers the waterfront on principles and techniques, and it is a handy source for leader education and development. Two companion pieces would be helpful: leading large organizations and leading a staff.

- *Becoming a Leader of Character: 6 Habits that Make or Break a Leader at Work and at Home* by James L. Anderson and Dave Anderson (New York: Morgan James Publishing, 2017). This compact, innovative book captures the essentials of character necessary for effective leadership. An inspirational resource for the study of leadership in any setting.

Leadership Concepts and Insights

- *Rules and Tools for Leaders: From Developing Your Own Skills to Running Organizations of Any Size, Practical Advice for Leaders at All Levels*, 4th Edition, by Perry M. Smith, MG, USAF (Ret.) and Jeffrey W. Foley BG, USA (Ret.) (New York: A Perigee Book, 2013). The authors know and share a lot about the nitty and gritty of learning and leading in large organizations. Wonderfully relevant advice on every page.
- *Taking Charge: A Practical Guide for Leaders* by Perry M. Smith (Washington, DC: National Defense University Press, 1986). If there is a companion piece to *A Military Leadership Notebook*, this is it. If you want more advice on leading, a quick review of personality types, and some perennially useful checklists, this is the place.
- *Ambition: How We Manage Success and Failure Throughout Our Lives* (Gilbert Brim. New York: Basic Books, 1992). A pertinent discussion on understanding the human drives leading to an understanding of self and others. Bert Brim a wise man and a good writer. "Ambition" we all need to confront.
- "What We Know About Leadership" by R. Hogan, G. Curphy, and J. Hogan (*American Psychologist* vol. 49, no. 6, June 1994). A great place to start when exploring definitions, basic constructs, and lingering issues.

- *If I'm In Charge Here, Why Is Everybody Laughing?* by David P. Campbell (Greensboro, NC: Center for Creative Leadership, 1994). A lively exploration of leadership by a creative personality.
- *The CCL Guide to Leadership in Action: How Managers and Organizations Can Improve the Practice of Leadership*, edited by Martin Wilcox and Stephen Rush (Greensboro, NC: Center for Creative Leadership, 2004). A convenient introduction to a variety of techniques for organizational leaders.
- *The Future of the Army Profession: Second Edition* by Don M. Snider and Lloyd J. Matthews (Boston: McGraw-Hill 2005). This definitive collection of diverse perspectives on military culture addresses about every issue that confronts professional soldiers. A unique resource.
- *Leadership: Enhancing the Lessons of Experience, Third Edition* by Richard L. Hughes, Robert C. Ginnett, and Gordon J. Curphy (Boston: Irwin/McGraw-Hill. 1999). This is a textbook that explains comfortably the primary concepts and studies driving leader education. It is "academic," but a great reference for those wanting to probe the links between theory and practice.
- *The Officers' Guide, 17th Edition* (Harrisburg, PA: The Military Service Publishing Co., 1951). It makes more sense now than when I quickly skipped over it in 1952. A hard book to locate, but a real gem. It reveals changes in protocol but consistency in professional values.
- *On Becoming a Leader: The Leadership Classic. Revised and Updated* by Warren Bennis (New York: Basic Books, 2009). A revision of the 1989 version, still packed with crisp wisdom from the expert who said Fort Benning provided more help with leadership than did Harvard or MIT.
- *A New Paradigm of Leadership: An Inquiry into Transformational Leadership* by B. M. Bass (Washington, DC: U.S. Army Research Institute for the Behavioral and Social Sciences, 1996). A good interpretation of transactional and transformational leadership and how those concepts are relevant to military leadership education and practice.

- *The Leadership Triad: Knowledge, Trust, and Power* by Dale Zand (New York: Oxford University Press, 1997). A real winner; the section on "trust" alone is worth the price.

Tactical Leadership in Korea, Vietnam, and Post 9/11

- *Platoon Leader: A Memoir of Command in Combat* by James R. McDonough (New York: Presidio Press, 1985). This candid memoir spells out how a competent, thoughtful, and courageous junior leader acts and feels at the cutting edge of the military.
- *The Only Thing Worth Dying For* by Eric Blehm (Sanford, NC: Collins, 2010). This coverage of small unit action in Afghanistan has leadership and organizational behavior examples on every page. It explains how American soldiers can innovate and win if given latitude and support.
- *Forgotten: Ideological Conflicts in Korea, Vietnam, Iraq, and Afghanistan* by Sam C. Holliday (Alpharetta, GA: BOOKLOGIX, 2014). This powerful description of war in Korea is breathtaking. The rare mix of tactical and strategic, philosophy and politics, personal and societal brings a cold blast of reality to any leadership discussion.
- *Combat Recon: My year with the ARVN* by Robert D. Parrish. (New York: St. Martin's Press, 1991.) This intimate, candid record of service as an advisor to Vietnamese Army units shows combat leadership, versatility, and innovation at its best. I may be biased toward this book because so much of my time was spent with Army of Vietnam organizations.
- *Ramadi Unclassified: A Roadmap to Peace in the Most Dangerous City in Iraq* by Anthony E. Deane (Bay Village, Ohio: Praetorian Books, 2016). This remarkable work of an insightful and competent commander reveals the complexity of contemporary operations and the thoughtful and innovative leadership that contemporary commanders provide in response.

- *We Were Soldiers Once ... and Young: Ia Drang-the Battle That Changed the War in Vietnam* by Harold G. Moore and Joseph L. Galloway (New York: Random House, 1992). This classic covers the essence of combat leadership anywhere, any time.

Strategic Viewpoints

- *Fighting the Cold War: A Soldier's Memoir* by John R. Galvin (Lexington, KY: University Press of Kentucky, 2015). General Galvin's tome deserves a place alongside Grant's memoirs. It is a forthright portrayal by one of America's most gifted and consequential twentieth century figures.
- *Honorable Warrior: General Harold K. Johnson and the Ethics of Command* by Lewis Sorley (Lawrence, KS: University of Kansas Press, 1998). A depiction of the ethical dilemmas faced by one of America's truly heroic soldiers. Its lessons are timeless.
- *Executive Leadership: A Practical Guide to Managing Complexity* by Elliott Jacques and Stephen Clement (Hoboken, NJ: Wiley-Blackwell, 1994). If you want to explore deep concepts aimed at leading complex organizations, this is a great place to start.
- *Jacob L. Devers: A General's Life* by James Scott Wheeler (Lexington, KY: The University Pres of Kentucky, 2015). The primary lesson here is that personal relationships and personal biases matter. It should remind senior leaders that in meeting challenges of strategic leadership, self-awareness is a powerful ally. A first-rate, enjoyable contribution to World War II scholarship.
- *My Share of the Task: A Memoir* by Stanley McCrystal (New York: Penguin, 2013). This candid biography offers a close-up view of both tactical and strategic scenarios, revealing the unique complexities faced by contemporary senior military leaders. His *Team of Teams: New Rules of Engagement for a Complex World (2015)*

neatly merges managerial history with lessons from his extensive operational experience and provides compelling guidelines for executive leadership.

- *Hope Is Not a Method: What Business Leaders Can Learn from America's Military* by Gordon R. Sullivan and Michael V. Harper (New York: Broadway Books, 1996). This bestseller describes a commonsense approach to adapting large, complex organizations to contemporary realities. It is jammed with ideas from active leaders about how to get the job done amid economic, political, and military change.
- *Marshall: A Statesman Shaped in the Crucible of War.* Rachel Yarnell Thompson. (Leesburg, VA: George C. Marshall Center, Inc. 2014). A marvelous review of the life of the most impactful American military leader of the twentieth century.
- *The Mask of Command* by John Keegan (New York: Penguin Books, 1987). No listing of references on leadership would be complete without this classic. Tales of Alexander, Wellington, Grant, and Hitler reveal timeless lessons for professional officers.
- *Partners in Command: George Marshall and Dwight Eisenhower in War and Peace* by Mark Perry (New York: Penguin Books, 2007). Wonderful insights of World War II personalities and how their styles, ambitions, and competencies contributed to ultimate victory. A nice companion to the insights of Wheeler's biography of Jacob Devers.

Collections

- *Leadership: The Warrior's Art* by Christopher Kolenda, author and editor (Carlisle Barracks, PA: The Army War College Foundation Press, 2001). This collection provides insights from a remarkable set of scholars and practitioners on a broad array of leadership topics.
- *Military Leadership in Pursuit of Excellence, Fourth Edition* edited by Robert L. Taylor and William E. Rosenbach (Boulder, CO: Westview, 2000). There are

newer editions of this paperback summary of leadership articles (sixth edition published in 2009). I am biased toward this one. It includes an excellent mix of both timeless (Ridgway) and contemporary (Sashkin and Rosenbach) notions about leading.

CPSIA information can be obtained
at www.ICGtesting.com
Printed in the USA
BVOW07s1423181217
503089BV00029B/536/P